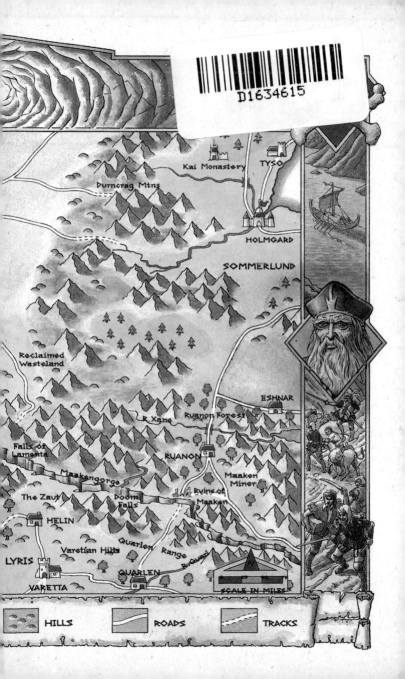

 he bearer of
this scroll,

name _Jae Jong Nomura_

is a _OX_

in the Order of the Kai

# THE LEGACY OF VASHNA

## THE AUTHOR

JOE DEVER was born in 1956 at Woodford Bridge in Essex. After he left college, he became a professional musician, working in studios in Europe and America. While working in Los Angeles in 1977, he discovered a game called 'Dungeons and Dragons' and was soon an enthusiastic player. Five years later he won the Advanced Dungeons and Dragons Championships in the US, where he was the only British competitor. The award-winning Lone Wolf adventures are the culmination of many years of developing the world of Magnamund. They are printed in several languages and sold throughout the world. In 1990 he was awarded an International Cultural Diploma of Honour by the American Biographical Institute, in recognition of his outstanding contribution to fantasy literature.

Joe also writes for modelling journals and contributes to Britain's leading role-playing games magazines.

LONE WOLF 16

# THE LEGACY OF VASHNA

Joe Dever

Illustrated by Brian Williams
Cover by Peter Jones

RED FOX

A Red Fox Book
Published by Random Century Children's Books
20 Vauxhall Bridge Road, London SW1V 2SA

A division of Random Century Group
London Melbourne Sydney Auckland
Johannesburg and agencies throughout the world

First published by Red Fox 1991
Text © Joe Dever 1991
Illustrations © Brian Williams 1991

Set in Souvenir Light
by JH Graphics Ltd, Reading, Berks

Printed and bound in Great Britain
by Cox & Wyman Ltd, Reading, Berks

ISBN 0 09 986050 3

*To Margaret Foden*

## GRAND MASTER DISCIPLINES NOTES

| 1 |
|---|
| 2 |
| 3 |
| 4 |
| 5 5th Grand Master Discipline if you have completed 1 Grand Master adventure successfully |
| 6 6th Grand Master Discipline if you have completed 2 Grand Master adventures successfully |

| BACKPACK (max. 10 articles) | MEALS |
|---|---|
| 1 3 Rope | -12 |
| 2 Potion | |
| 3 Tinder Box | |
| 4 2 Bottle of Wine | |
| 5 Comb | —3 EP if no Meal available when instructed to eat. |
| 6 Pipe | BELT POUCH Containing Gold Crowns (50 maximum) |
| 7 myglass | 50 |
| 8 Blowpipe | |
| 9 small sack | (6) |
| 10 | |

CS = COMBAT SKILL   EP = ENDURANCE POINTS

# ACTION CHART

| COMBAT SKILL | ENDURANCE POINTS |
|---|---|
| ~~14:1~~ 50 | 50 |
| | 0 = dead |

## COMBAT RECORD

| ENDURANCE POINTS | | ENDURANCE POINTS |
|---|---|---|
| LONE WOLF | COMBAT RATIO | ENEMY |
| LONE WOLF | COMBAT RATIO | ENEMY |
| LONE WOLF | COMBAT RATIO | ENEMY |
| LONE WOLF | COMBAT RATIO | ENEMY |
| LONE WOLF | COMBAT RATIO | ENEMY |

| GRAND MASTER RANK |
|---|
| |

# SPECIAL ITEMS LIST

| DESCRIPTION | KNOWN EFFECTS |
|---|---|
| Black Token | Protection |
| Hexagonal Token | |

# WEAPONS LIST

## WEAPONS (maximum 2 Weapons)

| 1 | 2 Bow |
|---|-------|
| 2 | 2 Broad sword |

If holding Weapon and appropriate Grand Weaponmastery
in combat + 3CS

## GRAND WEAPONMASTERY CHECKLIST

| | | | |
|---|---|---|---|
| DAGGER | +5 | SPEAR | |
| MACE | | SHORT SWORD | B |
| WARHAMMER | | BOW | +5 |
| AXE | 2 | SWORD | 1 |
| QUARTERSTAFF | 2 | BROADSWORD | 3 |

## QUIVER & ARROWS

| Quiver | No. of arrows carried |
|--------|----------------------|
| ✓ YES/NO  6 | 32 |

# THE STORY SO FAR . . .

You are Grand Master Lone Wolf, last of the Kai Lords of Sommerlund and sole survivor of a massacre that wiped out the First Order of your elite warrior caste.

It is the year MS 5077 and twenty-seven years have passed since your brave kinsmen perished at the hands of the Darklords of Helgedad. These champions of evil, who were sent forth by Naar, the King of the Darkness, to destroy the fertile world of Magnamund, have themselves since been destroyed. You vowed to avenge the murder of the Kai and you kept your pledge, for it was you who brought about their downfall when alone you infiltrated their foul domain — the Darklands — and caused the destruction of their leader, Archlord Gnaag, and the seat of his power that was the infernal city of Helgedad.

In the wake of their destruction, chaos befell the Darkland armies who, until then, had been poised to conquer all of Magnamund. Some factions which comprised this huge army, most notably the barbaric Drakkarim, began to fight with the others for control. This disorder quickly escalated into an all-out civil war, which allowed the free-state armies of Magnamund time in which to recover and launch a counter-offensive. Skilfully their commanders exploited the chaos and secured a swift and total victory over an enemy far superior in numbers.

For seven years now peace has reigned in Sommerlund. Under your direction, the once-ruined monastery of the Kai has been thoroughly rebuilt and restored to its former glory, and the task of teaching a Second Order of Kai warriors the skills and proud traditions of your ancestors is also well under way. The new generation of Kai recruits, all of whom were born during the era of war against the Darklords, possess latent Kai skills and show exceptional promise. These skills will be nurtured and honed to perfection during their time at the Monastery so that they may teach and inspire future generations, thereby ensuring the continued security of your homeland in future years.

Your attainment of the rank of Kai Grand Master brought with it great rewards. Some, such as the restoration of the Kai and the undying gratitude of your fellow Sommlending, could have been anticipated. Yet there have also been rewards which you could not possibly have foreseen. The discovery that within you lay the potential to develop Kai Disciplines beyond those of the Magnakai, which, until now, were thought to be the ultimate that a Kai Master could aspire to, was truly a revelation. Your discovery has inspired you to set out upon a new and previously unknown path in search of the wisdom and power that no Kai lord before you has ever possessed. In the name of your creator, the God Kai, and for the greater glory of Sommerlund and the Goddess Ishir, you have vowed to reach the very pinnacle of Kai perfection — to attain all of the Grand Master Disciplines and become the first Kai Supreme Master.

With diligence and determination you set about the restoration of the Kai Monastery and organized the training of the Second Order recruits. Your efforts were soon rewarded and, within the space of two short years, the first raw recruits had graduated to become a cadre of gifted Kai Masters who, in turn, were able to commence the teaching of their skills to subsequent intakes of Kai novices. Readily the Kai Masters rose to their new-found responsibilities, leaving you free to devote more of your time to the pursuit and perfection of the Grand Master Disciplines. During this period you also received expert tutelage in the ways of magic from two of your most trusted friends and advisors: Guildmaster Banedon, leader of the Brotherhood of the Crystal Star, and Lord Rimoah, speaker for the High Council of the Elder Magi.

In the deepest subterranean level of the Monastery, a hundred feet below the Tower of the Sun, you ordered the excavation and construction of a special vault. In this magnificent chamber wrought of granite and gold, you placed the seven Lorestones of Nyxator, the gems of Kai power which you had recovered during your quest for the Magnakai. It was here, bathed in the golden light of those radiant gems, that you spent countless hours in pursuit of perfection. Sometimes alone, sometimes in the company of your two able advisors — Banedon and Rimoah — you worked hard to develop your innate Grand Master Disciplines, and grasp the fundamental secrets of Left-handed and Old Kingdom magic. During this time you noticed many remarkable changes taking place within your body: you became

13

physically and mentally stronger, your five primary senses sharpened beyond all that you had experienced before, and, perhaps most remarkably, your body began to age at a much slower rate. Now, for every five years that elapse you age but one year.

At this time many changes were occurring beyond the borders of Sommerlund. In the regions to the northeast of Magador and the Maakengorge, the Elder Magi of Dessi and the Herbwardens of Bautar were working together in an effort to restore the dusty volcanic wasteland to its former fertile state. It was the first tentative step towards the reclamation of all the Darklands. However, their progress was painfully slow, and both parties were resigned to the fact that their efforts to undo the damage caused by the Darklords would take centuries to complete.

Following the destruction of the Darklords of Helgedad, the Giaks, the most numerous of all Gnaag's troops, fled into the Darklands and sought refuge in the gigantic city-fortresses of Nadgazad, Aarnak, Gournen, Akagazad and Kaag. Within each of these hellish strongholds fierce fighting broke out as remnants of the Xaghash (lesser Darklords) and the Nadziranim (evil practitioners of Right-Handed Magic who once aided individual Darklord masters) fought for control. It is widely believed that by the time the Elder Magi and the Herbwardens reach the walls of these strongholds they will encounter no resistance; the occupants will have long since brought about their own extinction.

Elsewhere, throughout Northern Magnamund, peace reigns victorious and the peoples of the Free

Kingdoms rejoice in the knowledge that the age of the Darklords has finally come to an end. Readily men have exchanged their swords for hoes and their shields for ploughs, and now the only marching they do is along the ruts of their freshly furrowed fields. Few are the watchful eyes that scan the distant horizon in fear of what may appear, although there are still those who maintain their vigilance, for the agents of Naar come in many guises and there are those in Magnamund who wait quietly in the shadows for the chance to do his evil bidding.

Already your new-found skills have been tested against Naar's agents and you have, on each such occasion, acquitted yourself admirably. But your continuing victories against his minions have enraged the Dark God and rarely has his lust for vengeance been greater than it is at present. Recently, Lord Rimoah has counselled you to be extra vigilant for he fears that Naar is getting ready to strike at Sommerlund anew. The Elder Magi have received warnings from President Kadharian of Magador that something strange is taking place in the north of his country, in the mountainous territory which borders upon the Maakengorge. Freak storms and unseasonal weather have swept this remote region, and the night skies over Lake Vorndarol have, for several weeks now, been illuminated by eerie, inexplicable lights.

Lord Rimoah fears that Naar is plotting to revive Vashna, the greatest of all the Darklords, whose spirit is trapped deep within the fathomless reaches of the Maakengorge. It has remained there, in uneasy entombment, ever since the day the Darklord was

15

defeated in battle by King Ulnar I of Sommerlund. Vashna's body, and those of his loathsome troops, was hurled into the abyss, hopefully never to be seen again. Legend has it that the Darklord's body was destroyed but his spirit still lives on. He is said to be awaiting the day when he shall be made to rise, at the head of a vast army of undead warriors, and set loose to wreak his revenge upon Sommerlund and the house of Ulnar.

'If it is Naar's intention to resurrect Vashna and his army from the depths of the Maakengorge,' said an anxious Lord Rimoah, as you and he discussed the situation in the secure privacy of your vault below the Kai Monastery, 'then no free realm upon the face of Magnamund will be safe. It has always been Sommerlund's misfortune that Ulnar's victory over Vashna was never total. I have always feared that the legacy of the Maakengorge would one day awaken and confront us . . . and I fear, unless we act swiftly, that that day is about to dawn.'

For several hours, you and your learned advisor deliberated what could be done to prevent such a catastrophe. You decided that the exact nature of the threat had first to be determined if you were to combat it effectively. You were confident that your Grand Master Disciplines would enable you to unravel this mystery quickly and so you volunteered to journey to northern Magador and investigate the strange incidents at first hand. After all, there could be a perfectly innocent explanation for them.

'Let us hope it is so, Grand Master,' said Lord Rimoah, earnestly, 'but, nevertheless, do not forget what could confront you there. I shall pray to Kai and

Ishir to watch over and guide you on the journey ahead, Lone Wolf, and bring you home, swiftly, safely and victoriously.'

# THE GAME RULES

You keep a record of your adventure on the *Action Chart* that you will find in the front of this book. For ease of use, and for further adventuring , it is recommended that you photocopy these pages.

For more than six years, ever since the demise of the Darklords of Helgedad, you have devoted yourself to developing further your fighting prowess — COMBAT SKILL — and physical stamina — ENDURANCE. Before you begin this Grand Master adventure you need to measure how effective your training has been. To do this, take a pencil and, with your eyes closed, point with the blunt end of it on to the *Random Number Table* on the last page of the book. If you pick a *0* it counts as zero.

The first number that you pick from the *Random Number Table* in this way represents your COMBAT SKILL. Add 25 to the number you picked and write the total in the COMBAT SKILL section of your *Action Chart* (ie, if your pencil fell on the number *6* in the *Random Number Table* you would write in a COMBAT SKILL of 31). When you fight, your COMBAT SKILL will be pitted against that of your enemy. A high score in this section is therefore very desirable.

The second number that you pick from the *Random Number Table* represents your powers of ENDURANCE. Add 30 to this number and write the total in the ENDURANCE section of your *Action Chart* (ie, if your pencil fell on the number 7 on the *Random Number Table* you would have 37 ENDURANCE points).

If you are wounded in combat you will lose ENDURANCE points. If at any time your ENDURANCE points fall to zero, you are dead and the adventure is over. Lost ENDURANCE points can be regained during the course of the adventure, but your number of ENDURANCE points cannot rise above the number you have when you start an adventure.

**If you have successfully completed any of the previous adventures in the Lone Wolf series (Books 1–15), you can carry your current scores of COMBAT SKILL and ENDURANCE points over to Book 16. These scores may include Weapon-mastery, Curing and Psi-surge bonuses obtained upon completion of Lone Wolf Kai (Books 1–5) or Magnakai (Books 6–12) adventures. Only if you have completed these previous adventures will you benefit from the appropriate bonuses in the course of the Grand Master series. You may also carry over any Weapons and Backpack Items you had in your possession at the end of your last adventure, and these should be entered on your new Grand Master *Action Chart* (you are still limited to two Weapons, but you may now carry up to ten Backpack Items).**

However, only the following Special Items may be carried over from the Lone Wolf Kai (Books 1–5) and Magnakai (Books 6–12) series to the Lone Wolf Grand Master series (Books 13–onwards):

Crystal Star Pendant    Jewelled Mace
Sommerswerd    Silver Bow of Duadon
Silver Helm    Helshezag
Dagger of Vashna    Kagonite Chainmail

# KAI & MAGNAKAI DISCIPLINES

During your distinguished rise to the rank of Kai Grand Master, you have become proficient in all of the basic Kai and Magnakai Disciplines. These Disciplines have provided you with a formidable arsenal of natural abilities which have served you well in the fight against the agents and champions of Naar, King of the Darkness. A brief summary of your skills is given below.

**Weaponmastery**
Proficiency with all close combat and missile weapons. Master of unarmed combat; no COMBAT SKILL loss when fighting bare-handed.

## Animal Control
Communication with most animals; limited control over hostile creatures. Can use woodland animals as guides and can block a non-sentient creature's sense of taste and smell.

## Curing
Steady restoration of lost ENDURANCE points (to self and others) as a result of combat wounds. Neutralization of poisons, venoms and toxins. Repair of serious battle wounds.

## Invisibility
Mask body heat and scent; hide effectively; mask sounds during movement; minor alterations of physical appearance.

## Huntmastery
Effective hunting of food in the wild; increased agility; intensified vision, hearing, smell and night vision.

## Pathsmanship
Read languages, decipher symbols, read footprints and tracks. Intuitive knowledge of compass points; detection of enemy ambush up to 500 metres; ability to cross terrain without leaving tracks; converse with sentient creatures; mask self from psychic spells of detection.

## Psi-surge
Attack enemies using the powers of the mind; set up disruptive vibrations in objects; confuse enemies.

## Psi-screen
Defence against hypnosis, supernatural illusions,

charms, hostile telepathy and evil spirits. Ability to divert and re-channel hostile psychic energy.

**Nexus**
Move small items by projection of mind power; withstand extremes of temperature; extinguish fire by force of will; limited immunity to flames, toxic gases and corrosive liquids.

**Divination**
Sense imminent danger; detect invisible or hidden enemy; telepathic communication; recognize magic-using and/or magical creatures; detect psychic residues; limited ability to leave body and spirit-walk.

# GRAND MASTER DISCIPLINES

Now, through the pursuit of new skills and the further development of your innate Kai abilities, you have set out upon a path of discovery that no other Kai Grand Master has ever attempted with success. Your determination to become the first Kai Supreme Master, by acquiring total proficiency in all twelve of the Grand Master Disciplines, is an awe-inspiring challenge. You will be venturing into the unknown, pushing back the boundaries of human limitation in the pursuit of greatness and the cause of Good. May the blessings of the gods Kai and Ishir go with you as you begin your brave and noble quest.

In the years following the demise of the Darklords you have reached the rank of Kai Grand Defender, which means that you have mastered *four* of the Grand Master Disciplines listed below. It is up to you to choose which four Disciplines these are. As all of the Grand Master Disciplines will be of use to you at some point during your adventure, pick your four skills with care. The correct use of a Grand Master Discipline at the right time could save your life.

When you have chosen your four Disciplines, enter them in the Grand Master Disciplines section of your *Action Chart*.

**Grand Weaponmastery**
This Discipline enables a Grand Master to become supremely efficient in the use of all weapons. When you enter combat with one of your Grand Master weapons, you add 5 points to your COMBAT SKILL. The rank of Kai Grand Defender, with which you begin the Grand Master series, means you are skilled in *two* of the weapons listed opposite and overleaf.

SPEAR

DAGGER

22

MACE

SHORT SWORD

WARHAMMER

BOW

QUARTERSTAFF

BROADSWORD

AXE

SWORD

**Animal Mastery**
Grand Masters have considerable control over hostile, non-sentient creatures. Also, they have the ability to converse with birds and fishes, and use them as guides.

**Deliverance** *(Advanced Curing)*
Grand Masters are able to use their healing power to repair serious battle wounds. If, while in combat, their COMBAT SKILL is reduced to 8 points or less, they can draw upon their mastery to restore 20 ENDURANCE points. This ability can only be used once every 20 days.

**Assimilance** *(Advanced Invisibility)*
Grand Masters are able to effect striking changes to their physical appearance, and maintain these changes over a period of a few days. They have also mastered advanced camouflage techniques that make them virtually undetectable in an open landscape.

**Grand Huntmastery**
Grand Masters are able to see in total darkness, and have greatly heightened senses of touch and taste.

**Grand Pathsmanship**
Grand Masters are able to resist entrapment by hostile plants, and have a super-awareness of ambush, or the threat of ambush, in woods and dense forests.

**Kai-surge**
When using their psychic ability to attack an enemy, Grand Masters may add 8 points to their COMBAT SKILL. For every round in which Kai-surge is used, Grand Masters need only deduct 1 ENDURANCE point. When using the weaker psychic attack — Mind-blast — they may add 4 points without loss of ENDURANCE points. (Kai-surge, Psi-surge and Mind-blast cannot be used simultaneously.)

Grand Masters cannot use Kai-surge if their ENDURANCE score falls to 6 points or below.

**Kai-screen**
In psychic combat, Grand Masters are able to construct mind fortresses capable of protecting themselves and others. The strength and capacity of these fortresses increases as a Grand Master advances in rank.

## Grand Nexus
Grand Masters are able to withstand contact with harmful elements, such as flames and acids, for upwards of an hour in duration. This ability increases as a Grand Master advances in rank.

## Telegnosis *(Advanced Divination)*
This Discipline enables a Grand Master to spirit-walk for far greater lengths of time, and with far fewer ill effects. Duration, and the protection of his inanimate body, increases as a Grand Master advances in rank.

## Magi-Magic
Under the tutelage of Lord Rimoah, you have been able to master the rudimentary skills of battle magic, as taught to the Vakeros — the native warriors of Dessi. As you advance in rank, so will your knowledge and mastery of Old Kingdom magic increase.

## Kai-alchemy
Under the tutelage of Guildmaster Banedon, you have mastered the elementary spells of Left-handed Magic, as practised by the Brotherhood of the Crystal Star. As you advance in rank, so will your knowledge and mastery of Left-handed magic increase, enabling you to craft new Kai weapons and artefacts.

If you successfully complete the mission as set in Book 16 of the Lone Wolf Grand Master series, you may add a further Grand Master Discipline of your choice to your *Action Chart* in Book 17.

For every Grand Master Discipline you possess, in excess of the original four Disciplines you begin with, you may add 1 point to your basic COMBAT SKILL score and 2 points to your basic ENDURANCE points score. These bonus points, together with your extra Grand Master Discipline(s), your original four Grand Master Disciplines, and any Special Items that you have found and been able to keep during your adventures, may then be carried over and used in the next Grand Master adventure, which is called

*The Deathlord of Ixia.*

## EQUIPMENT

Before you set off on your long journey to Magador you take with you a map of the area (see the inside front cover of this book) and a pouch of gold. To find out how much gold is in the pouch, pick a number from the *Random Number Table* and add 20 to the number you have picked. The total equals the number of Gold Crowns inside the pouch, and you should now enter this number in the 'Gold Crowns' section of your *Action Chart*.

**If you have successfully completed any of the previous Lone Wolf adventures (Books 1–15), you may add this sum to the total sum of Crowns you already possess. Fifty Crowns is the maximum you can carry, but additional Crowns can be left in safe-keeping at your Monastery.**

**You can take four items from the list below, again adding to these, if necessary, any you may already possess from previous adventures (remember, you are still limited to two Weapons, but you may now carry a maximum of ten Backpack Items).**

SWORD (Weapons)

BOW (Weapons)

QUIVER (Special Items) This contains six arrows; record them on your Weapons List.

AXE (Weapons)

2 MEALS (Meals) Each Meal takes up one space in your Backpack.

ROPE (Backpack Item)

POTION OF LAUMSPUR (Backpack Item) This potion restores 4 ENDURANCE points to your total when swallowed after combat. There is enough for only one dose.

QUARTERSTAFF (Weapons)

DAGGER (Weapons)

List the four items that you choose on your *Action Chart*, under the appropriate headings, and make a note of any effect it may have on your ENDURANCE points or COMBAT SKILL.

## Equipment – how to use it

*Weapons*
The maximum number of weapons that you can carry is *two*. Weapons aid you in combat. If you have the Grand Master Discipline of Grand Weaponmastery and a correct weapon, it adds 3 points to your COMBAT SKILL. If you find a weapon during your adventure, you may pick it up and use it.

*Bows and Arrows*
During your adventure there will be opportunities to use a bow and arrow. If you equip yourself with this weapon, and you possess at least one arrow, you may use it when the text of a particular section allows you to do so. The bow is a useful weapon, for it enables you to hit an enemy at a distance. However, a bow cannot be used in hand-to-hand combat, therefore it is strongly recommended that you also equip yourself with a close combat weapon, such as a sword or an axe.

In order to use a bow you must possess a quiver and at least one arrow. Each time the bow is used, erase an arrow from your *Action Chart*. A bow cannot, of course, be used if you exhaust your supply of arrows, but the opportunity may arise during your adventure for you to replenish your stock of arrows.

If you have the Discipline of Grand Weaponmastery with a bow, you may add 3 points to any number that you pick from the *Random Number Table*, when using the bow.

## Backpack Items

These must be stored in your Backpack. Because space is limited, you may keep a maximum of ten articles, including Meals, in your Backpack at any one time. You may only carry one Backpack at a time. During your travels you will discover various useful items which you may decide to keep. You may exchange or discard them at any point when you are not involved in combat.

Any item that may be of use, and which can be picked up on your adventure and entered on your *Action Chart* is given either initial capitals (eg Gold Dagger, Magic Pendant), or is clearly labelled as a Backpack Item. Unless you are told that it is a Special Item, carry it in your Backpack.

## Special Items

Special Items are not carried in the Backpack. When you discover a Special Item, you will be told how or where to carry it. The maximum number of Special Items that can be carried on any adventure is twelve.

## Food

Food is carried in your Backpack. Each Meal counts as one item. You will need to eat regularly during your adventure. If you do not have any food when you are instructed to eat a Meal, you will lose 3 ENDURANCE points. However, if you have chosen the Discipline of Grand Huntmastery, you will not need to tick off a Meal when instructed to eat.

*Potion of Laumspur*
This is a healing potion that can restore 4 ENDURANCE points to your total when swallowed after combat. There is enough for one dose only. If you discover any other potion during the adventure, you will be informed of its effect. All potions are Backpack Items.

# RULES FOR COMBAT

There will be occasions during your adventure when you have to fight an enemy. The enemy's COMBAT SKILL and ENDURANCE points are given in the text. Lone Wolf's aim in the combat is to kill the enemy by reducing his ENDURANCE points to zero while losing as few ENDURANCE points as possible himself.

At the start of a combat, enter Lone Wolf's and the enemy's ENDURANCE points in the appropriate boxes on the 'Combat Record' section of your *Action Chart*.

The sequence for combat is as follows:

1. Add any extra points gained through your Grand Master Disciplines and Special Items to your current COMBAT SKILL total.

2. Subtract the COMBAT SKILL of your enemy from this total. The result is your *Combat Ratio*. Enter it on the *Action Chart*.

**Example**
Lone Wolf (COMBAT SKILL 32) is attacked by a pack of Doomwolves (COMBAT SKILL 30). He is taken by surprise and is not given the opportunity of evading their attack. Lone Wolf has the Grand

Master Discipline of Kai-surge to which the Doom-wolves are not immune, so Lone Wolf adds 3 points to his COMBAT SKILL, giving him a total COMBAT SKILL of 35.

He subtracts the Doomwolf pack's COMBAT SKILL from his own, giving a *Combat Ratio* of +5. (35 − 30 = +5). +5 is noted on the *Action Chart* as the *Combat Ratio*.

3. When you have your *Combat Ratio*, pick a number from the *Random Number Table*.

4. Turn to the COMBAT RESULTS TABLE on the inside back cover of this book. Along the top of the chart are shown the *Combat Ratio* numbers. Find the number that is the same as your *Combat Ratio* and cross-reference it with the random number that you have picked (the random numbers appear on the side of the chart). You now have the number of ENDURANCE points lost by both Lone Wolf and his enemy in this round of combat. (*E* represents points lost by the enemy; *LW* represents points lost by Lone Wolf.)

**Example**
The *Combat Ratio* between Lone Wolf and the Doomwolf Pack has been established as +5. If the number taken from the *Random Number Table* is a *2*, then the result of the first round of combat is:

Lone Wolf loses 3 ENDURANCE points (plus an additional 1 point for using Kai-surge).
Doomwolf Pack loses 7 ENDURANCE points.

5. On the *Action Chart*, mark the changes in ENDURANCE points to the participants in the combat.

6. Unless otherwise instructed, or unless you have an option to evade, the next round of combat now starts.

7. Repeat the sequence from Stage 3.

This process of combat continues until ENDURANCE points of either the enemy or Lone Wolf are reduced to zero, at which point the one with the zero score is declared dead. If Lone Wolf is dead, the adventure is over. If the enemy is dead, Lone Wolf proceeds but with his ENDURANCE points reduced.

**A summary of Combat Rules appears on the page after the *Random Number Table*.**

**Evasion of combat**
During your adventure you may be given the chance to evade combat. If you have already engaged in a round of combat and decide to evade, calculate the combat for that round in the usual manner. All points lost by the enemy as a result of that round are ignored, and you make your escape. Only Lone Wolf may lose ENDURANCE points during that round (but then that is the risk of running away!). You may only evade if the text of the particular section allows you to do so.

# GRAND MASTER'S WISDOM

Northern Magador, which borders upon the Maakengorge, is a notoriously wild and treacherous region. Be wary and on your guard at all times, for you can expect little help from the outlaws and fell creatures who dwell in this area.

Some of the things that you will encounter during your mission will be of use to you in this and future Lone Wolf books, while others may be red herrings of no real value at all. If you discover any items, be selective in what you choose to keep.

Pick your four Grand Master Disciplines with care, for a wise choice will enable any player to complete the mission, no matter how weak their initial COMBAT SKILL and ENDURANCE scores may be. Successful completion of previous Lone Wolf adventures, although an advantage, is not essential for the completion of this Grand Master adventure.

May the light of Kai and Ishir be your guide as you venture into the unknown.

For Sommerlund and the Kai!

# IMPROVED GRAND MASTER DISCIPLINES

As you rise through the higher levels of Kai Grand Mastery, you will find that your Disciplines will steadily improve. For example, if you possess the Discipline of Grand Nexus when you reach the Grand Master rank of Grand Thane, you will be able to pass freely through Shadow Gates and explore the nether realms of Aon and the Daziarn Plane.

If you are a Grand Master who has reached the rank of Sun Lord, you will now benefit from improvements to the following Grand Master Disciplines:

## Grand Weaponmastery
Sun Lords with this Discipline are able to cause the metal edge of any non-magical weapon to ignite and burn fiercely. When a weapon thus affected is used in combat, it inflicts an additional 1 ENDURANCE point loss upon an enemy in every successful round of combat. This ability cannot be used with a wholly wooden weapon such as a quarterstaff.

## Assimilance
Sun Lords who possess this skill are able to cause the outline of their bodies to become blurred and indistinct. By so doing, they can greatly increase their chances of avoiding magical and/or non-magical missiles directed at them.

## Grand Huntmastery
Kai Sun Lords with this skill are able to see, with acute accuracy, light in the infrared spectrum, ie. they can see complex patterns generated by heat in near or total

darkness. They can also see light in the ultraviolet spectrum.

## Kai Surge
Sun Lords who possess mastery of this Discipline are able to launch a Kai-Blast — a pulse of intense psychic energy which is capable of affecting both psychically active and inactive enemies. This form of psychic attack is very effective, more so than a usual Kai-surge, Psi-surge or Mindblast. It can cause an enemy to lose between 2 and 18 ENDURANCE points in one attack. However, use of a Kai-Blast will reduce a Sun Lord's ENDURANCE points total by 4. It cannot be used in conjunction with any other form of psychic attack.

## Telegnosis
Sun Lords who possess this Discipline are able to alter their body-weight in order to walk successfully upon different kinds of surface, eg: water, mud, lava and quicksand. Time duration and degree of surface difficulty increases as a Grand Master rises in rank.

## Magi-magic
Grand Masters who have reached the rank of Sun Lord are able to use the following battle-spells of the Elder Magi:

*Penetrate* — This increases the penetrative energy of any arrow, or arrow-like missile, launched by a Sun Lord.

*Energy Grasp* — This spell enables a Sun Lord to discharge a powerful electrical force into anything he or she touches. It is similar in effect to the Brotherhood spell 'Lightning Hand', but differs in that it is easier to control and channel the resulting energy. It also requires the actual touching of an object or an enemy to effect the spell.

The nature of any additional improvements and how they affect your Grand Master Disciplines will be noted in the 'Improved Grand Master Disciplines' section of future Lone Wolf books.

# LEVELS OF KAI GRAND MASTERSHIP

The following table is a guide to the rank and titles you can achieve at each stage of your journey along the road of Kai Grand Mastership. As you successfully complete each adventure in the Lone Wolf Grand Master series, you will gain an additional Grand Master Discipline and progress towards the pinnacle of Kai perfection — becoming a Kai Supreme Master.

| No. of Grand Master Disciplines acquired | Grand Master Rank |
|---|---|
| 1 | Kai Grand Master Senior |
| 2 | Kai Grand Master Superior |
| 3 | Kai Grand Sentinel |
| 4 | Kai Grand Defender — *You begin the Lone Wolf Grand Master adventures at this level of Mastery* |
| 5 | Kai Grand Guardian |
| 6 | Sun Knight |
| 7 | Sun Lord |
| 8 | Sun Thane |
| 9 | Grand Thane |
| 10 | Grand Crown |
| 11 | Sun Prince |
| 12 | Kai Supreme Master |

# 1

The hours leading up to your departure from the Kai Monastery are spent in the company of your able advisor, Lord Rimoah. Having discussed the mission at great length, you busy yourself now with the practical preparations for your long journey to Magador. He gives you a scroll which contains a written invitation from President Kadharian to attend his senate to 'discuss trade between Sommerlund and Magador'. It will provide a cover for you should the need arise to justify your journey. Also, in the interests of secrecy, you decide it best to discard your formal Kai robes in favour of less conspicuous garments, and you choose instead to wear the simple clothes of a guildsman — woollen breeches, leather tunic, and a cloak. Dressed thus, and aided by your innate Kai skills of invisibility, you feel confident you will be able to travel the road to Helgor, the Magadorian capital, without drawing undue attention to yourself or your purpose.

By horse, the journey to Helgor could be expected to take five weeks. Your initial thought had been to send word to your friend, Guildmaster Banedon, requesting that he allow you use of his magical skyship *Skyrider*. However, on this occasion you will have to forego the speedy comfort of his wondrous craft, for Banedon is using it himself on a quest to the distant land of Bhanar in southern Magnamund, and he is not expected to return to Sommerlund before the year's end.

**2**

Your second choice was also to prove unsuitable. Having resigned yourself to a long journey on horseback, you immediately sent an order to the monastery stables for your horse, Storm, to be saddled and made ready. This fine Slovarian stallion had been a gift to you from Elector Manatine of Palmyrion, in gratitude for the crucial part you played in the victory over the evil Cener Druids of Ruel. His strength, intelligence, and indomitable spirit had reminded you so much of your old Kai tutor — Storm Hawk — that you chose to name the horse Storm in his memory. But, as Rimoah quickly pointed out, such a magnificent horse would be sure to attract suspicion, especially if it was ridden by what appeared to be a humble guildsman. And so, albeit reluctantly, you had the stables prepare you another horse, a strong but less exceptional mount called Bracer.

Turn to **105**.

**2**

An ugly, one-eyed mongrel is standing in front of the inn, barking defiantly at the first-floor window through which you are observing the Vakovarians. You curse it under your breath and mentally you command it to go away, using your innate Kai skill of animal kinship. The hound ceases its infernal yapping and runs off, whimpering pathetically, but its noise has already attracted the unwanted attention of some brigands who are looting the ruins nearby. They surround and enter the ground floor of the inn, eager to discover what it was that made the dog run away so abruptly.

Pick a number from the *Random Number Table*. If you have the Grand Master Discipline of Assimilance, add 3 to the number you have picked.

If your total score is now *9* or less, turn to **329**. If it is *10* or more, turn to **211**.

**3**

The moment you slay the first two of these strange creatures, their bodies dissolve into a swirling cloud of steamy vapour. Now, upon the death of the third beast, the vapours unite and expand with breath-taking speed until the basalt island and the entire fiery plain beyond is engulfed by a thickening grey fog.

You walk through this sea of mist for what seems like an eternity until your senses detect that something is circling high above you. At first you suspect that more of the golden-winged creatures have come hunting for you, but then you detect that it is something completely different. There is only one creature, and you sense that it is using a highly-developed psychic probe in order to seek you out.

If you possess Grand Nexus, and have reached the Kai rank of Sun Knight, or higher, turn to **31**.

If you do not possess this skill, or if you have yet to attain this level of Kai mastery, turn to **106**.

## 4

One of the bolts hits your Backpack. The force of the impact lifts you off your feet and sends you tumbling backwards across the floor. (Erase three items from your Backpack List and reduce your ENDURANCE by 2 points.)

Turn to **157**.

## 5

You reach the cover of a dense pine copse and quickly dismount. Having secured Bracer's reins to a tree, you move to the edge of the copse to try to catch a glimpse of your attackers. You have no difficulty seeing them: a dozen brigands, armed with crossbows and swords, are rushing through the undergrowth towards your hiding place.

If you possess a Bow and wish to use it, turn to **330**.

If you do not, turn to **136**.

## 6

The instant you correctly complete the sequence, a deep hum resonates from inside the upper tier and slowly it opens to reveal a hexagonal crystal plinth with a circular hole at its centre. Your Kai senses inform you that by inserting the tip of the Deathstaff into the hole, you will cause the shadow gate beneath the great arch to close.

Trembling with fear and exhilaration, you raise the Deathstaff above your head and bring it down with one mighty thrust, driving it deep into the hole.

Turn to **246**.

## 7

You dive over the mounds of charred timbers, aiming to land in the cobblestoned street outside the hut, but the bolt hits the building whilst you are in mid-air and the force of the concussion sends you twisting away in another direction.

Pick a number from the *Random Number Table*. If you possess Grand Huntmastery, add 2 to the number you have picked. If you possess Grand Huntmastery *and* Assimilance, add another 2.

If your total score is now 6 or less, turn to **299**. If it is 7 or more, turn to **266**.

## 8

You have ridden to within five miles of the hamlet when you are forced to leave the trail and take cover. Ahead, you see a group of Vakovarian bandits encamped on a bridge which carries the trail across a fast-flowing stream. Rather than risk a confrontation, you follow this tributary of the River Storn a mile downstream until you happen upon a shallow bend where the water is fordable on horseback. You cross here, make a wide detour, and then return to the trail a mile beyond the Vakovarian's encampment.

**9**

The trail gradually descends towards the burnt and derelict hovels of Vorn, clustered in squalid disarray around a greystone quay. Vakovarian bandits occupy the ruined hamlet and you decide it wise to leave the trail in case they have posted a lookout. A copse of stunted firs offers you a good hiding place for your horse. You tether him here, then gather some grasses and roots for him to eat while you are away scouting the hamlet.

You have no difficulty entering Vorn unseen. From the first-floor ruins of a burnt-out inn on the outskirts of the hamlet you make a careful observation of the Vakovarians. They seem to be systematically looting the ruins and transporting their ill-gotten booty to a fishing boat which is moored at the quay. You are watching this boat closely when suddenly your concentration is broken by the sound of a yapping dog.

If you possess Animal Mastery, turn to **281**.
If you do not possess this Discipline, turn to **2**.

**9**

With weapon in hand you climb out of the window. You are expecting the archer to attack you the moment you appear but the balcony is deserted: he has disappeared. Then your keen eyes catch a glimpse of movement on the roof of a building opposite. It is the archer. He has leapt the narrow street from the rail of the balcony and he is now making his escape across the rooftops of the north quarter.

With the grace of a springing panther you leap from the balcony and land on the roof opposite. Without breaking your stride, you set off after the fleeing assassin and pursue him to the edge of a flat-topped warehouse at the end of Tavern Lane. Here a plank of wood had been laid down to span the gap of ten metres to the rooftop opposite. The man makes a sure-footed escape across the plank, then kicks it away to prevent you from following him.

If you are determined to follow him and wish to try to leap across the gap, turn to **42**.

If you do not wish to make the jump, turn to **191**.

### 10

Upon hearing you utter the correct solution to her riddle, Shamath recoils in horror. You have beaten her challenge and the humiliation she feels cuts her as sharply as any sword.

She begins to whimper. Then, quite suddenly, a geyser of flame shoots from the floor and engulfs her wormlike body. You watch with disbelief as the tendrilled flesh blackens and flakes away in a matter of seconds, to leave nothing but a coiled heap of glowing cinders.

Turn to **261**.

### 11

Cautiously you approach the circle of boulders, leading your frozen horse by the reins. Through a gap in the boulders you see a pack of eight ridge-backed jackals feeding on the carcass of a Durncrag scavenger, a vulture-like bird of prey. They are engrossed with their meal until they suddenly detect the scent of their most-favoured food: live horse-meat.

I. With a frenzied howl the wild jackals abandon the leathery carcass and come streaming through the gap in the boulders.

With a frenzied howl the wild jackals abandon the feathery carcass and come streaming through the gap in the boulders, drawn by the scent of your horse. They seem to know that he is in a weakened state and this fuels their fury. Your horse takes fright and tries to pull away, his hooves flailing the air perilously close to your skull and, as the first of the jackals makes its attack, you find yourself struggling to hold on to the reins with one hand and fight them off with the other.

Vorndarol jackals:
COMBAT SKILL 42      ENDURANCE 38

Unless you possess Grand Weaponmastery and have reached the rank of Sun Knight, or higher, you must reduce your COMBAT SKILL by 5 for the duration of this combat.

> You may evade combat after four rounds, by turning to **222**.
>
> If you win this fight, turn to **347**.

**12**

The first light of dawn brings with it a dramatic change in the weather. The storm has ended and the sky is now bright and clear, but on the distant horizon you can still see flashes of lightning and hear thunder rumbling in the mountains.

After drying out your equipment and tending to the minor cuts and abrasions that Bracer sustained last night, you climb into the saddle and set off along the muddy track, most of which you discover has been washed away by the flood. The damp earth is steaming in the unusual heat of the morning sun and the air crackles with an eerie residue of static electricity.

You continue your ride through the hills without stopping until, shortly after midday, you come to a derelict hovel which stands at the edge of a marshy peat bog. Your Kai senses inform you that there is somebody inside and, spurred on by curiosity, you resolve to find out who they are. You dismount and leave Bracer to feed on the marsh grass while you go forward to investigate the hovel on foot. You are six metres away from its rotting wooden door when suddenly it creaks open and you see an old man standing in the doorway. He is smiling at you.

If you have ever visited the city of Varetta, the city of Tahou, or a hut on the Ruanon Pike in a previous Lone Wolf adventure, turn to **220**.

If you have never visited any of these places, turn to **53**.

**13**

The man makes a slow, sure-footed descent to within three metres of where you are standing, during which time his weapon's sights never leave your chest. You can tell immediately that he is a skilled hunter and, judging by his furs and his beautifully crafted crossbow, he is a successful one too.

Your muscles are tense and coiled like springs, ready to propel you out of the path of his crossbow bolt in case he fires. But then he says something which makes you realize that, maybe, he has no intentions of killing you after all.

Turn to **340**.

## 14

You approach the brigand leader stealthily, without making a sound. As you draw closer, you hear him cursing the incompetence of his men and you see him beating his clenched fist on the trunk of the fallen bough in frustration. Then, without warning, he turns around to retrieve something from a satchel lying on the ground nearby and his keen eyes catch sight of you creeping up on him. In an instant his sword is in his hand. You rush forward and launch your attack but you have lost the element of surprise. As he parries your first blow, he screams for his men to come to his aid.

Vakovarian brigand captain:
COMBAT SKILL 33      ENDURANCE 32

You may evade this combat after two rounds, by turning to **312**.

If you win and the fight lasts five rounds or less, turn to **145**.

If you win and the fight lasts six rounds or more, turn to **25**.

**15**

Using your Kai mastery, you attempt to stop the creature dead in its tracks with a sharp psychic command. The beast shudders, its instincts confused, but it possesses an unusually strong will and you can sense that it may overcome your mental suggestion.

Pick a number from the *Random Number Table*. For every Grand Master rank you have attained above that of Kai Grand Defender, add 1 to the number you have picked.

If your total score is now 5 or less, turn to **336**.
If it is 6 or more, turn to **306**.

**16**

You flick your heel against Bracer's flank and urge him towards the dingy street. Here, only a few houses show any light, and this through the knotholes and cracks of their bolted shutters. At length you come to a junction illuminated by a solitary street lantern. You are trying to decide which way to turn when your eye is distracted by something moving in the shadows. From out of a darkened doorway steps a pale-skinned woman wrapped in a black velvet cloak, edged with scarlet silk.

''T'is no night to be out ridin',' she says, her voice syrupy and seductive, 'not less you be lookin' for company.'

You tell her you have no need for her company and turn your horse to leave, but suddenly you find yourself transfixed by the woman's eyes and unable to move. They seem unnaturally vibrant, as if filled with a flickering green fire; she is using magic in an attempt to charm you. Instinctively, you draw on your innate psychic Kai powers to try to dispel the charm, but her magic is unusually strong.

If you possess the Grand Master Discipline of Kai-screen, turn to **346**.

If you do not possess this skill, turn to **290**.

**17**

You make a slow descent to the clearing, trusting to your camouflage skills to keep you hidden as you move from one boulder to the next. You are less than ten metres from the carcass when you hear the faint scrape of leather on stone. You turn to look and a man's voice growls, 'Don't move!'

Standing between two boulders away to your left is a grey-bearded man, clad in furs and clutching a loaded crossbow. The weapon is pointing at your heart.

If you possess the Discipline of Telegnosis, and wish to use it, turn to **201**.

If you do not possess this skill, or choose not to use it, turn to **280**.

## 18

Beyond the plateau the trail descends steeply towards a thick pine wood. Milky-white pools of water punctuate this section of the track, some deceptively deep, making the descent difficult and tiring. By the time you reach the wood your horse is in need of rest.

You dismount to take the weight off his back and, as you gather his reins together, you notice that the flap of your Backpack is undone. On checking the contents you discover that one of your possessions is missing. (Erase the second item on your list of Backpack Items. If you have only one item on your list, erase that one instead.)

As soon as your horse is rested, you remount him and set off through the pine wood, heading east.

Turn to **300**.

## 19

The three phantoms swoop down into the trees as if to pursue the fleeing cats, but then they break off their attack and come speeding once more towards the mouth of the cave.

You sense a hostile psychic presence about them, an evil mind-energy which is growing stronger as they draw nearer. You use your Magnakai skills to erect a psi-screen to protect your mind, but they launch a sudden massive bolt of their energy which buckles your hasty shield: lose 3 ENDURANCE points.

Turn to **205**.

## 20

The instant you step through the archway you feel an electrifying jolt run through your body, and snake-like tendrils of blue-white energy writhe from the rim of the arch to the hilt of Vashna's Dagger. A gasp of astonishment arises from the acolytes, audible even above the howling wind.

'We have an intruder in our midst,' screams Cadak, levelling his wizard's staff at you accusingly. You fight the paralysing effect of the current and tug the dagger free of its scabbard. For a moment the current weakens as it is absorbed and neutralized by the dark blade's unholy energy, but then the tip of Cadak's staff ignites with a crimson flame and the current intensifies anew, numbing your limbs with its insidious effect.

Turn to **228**.

## 21

You enter the open doorway and the hubbub of laughter and conversation dies momentarily as all eyes turn to stare in your direction. They consider you for a few moments, then the chatter and noise begin anew and the eyes return to other matters. After descending a flight of steps to the sunken floor of the taproom, you make your way through the noisy crowd to the beer-soaked counter. A husky serving wench thuds a pewter tankard down on the bar before you and fills it with frothing ale.

II. A husky serving wench thuds a pewter tankard down on the bar before you.

'First one's on the 'ouse,' she says, with a snarl, 'the rest y' pays for, understand?' You nod your reply and, as you sip the watery brew, you take stock of the inn's villainous clientele. They are not a pretty crowd. The Crooked Sage is a tavern with an ill reputation, even in the brawling turmoil of Helgor's north quarter. The city guard never patrol here; a weekly donation to the guard captain guarantees that they are always somewhere else. Order, and what passes for law, is kept by Chegga, the owner of the inn, and his two brutish sons — Zhola and Gorgan.

You finish your ale and the serving wench returns to refill your tankard.

'That'll be one Gold Crown,' she says, thrusting out a calloused palm. You place the crown on the bar and, as she goes to pick it up, you take hold of her wrist to prevent her from moving away.

'Where's Smudd? Is he here tonight?' you ask.

'Over there,' she growls, pointing to a shadowy alcove at the rear of the taproom, 'now let go o' me or I'll call Chegga.'

Calmly you release her, take up your ale, and walk slowly towards the place where Smudd is seated. He is in the company of a giggling bar-girl and does not notice that you are standing beside him until you thump your tankard down on his table. The sound startles him and immediately he reaches for his sword.

He has a desperate look about him which reminds you of a cornered rat. If you are to avoid a confrontation, you must do or say something to assuage his fear.

If you possess Kai-alchemy, turn to **294**.
If you wish to offer him some money, turn to **169**.
If you choose to offer him one of your Backpack Items, turn to **108**.

### 22

The Elder's suspicion swiftly turns to anger. He grabs your robe and pulls it open, revealing your leather tunic and breeches. Recognizing them at once to be Sommlending in origin, he gasps with shock as he guesses at your true identity.

Turn to **314**.

### 23

The cave offers adequate protection but you are plagued by a feeling of unease. A familiar tingling sensation runs up and down your spine; it is your sixth sense, warning you that danger lurks close by. You stand in the mouth of the cave and scan the surrounding storm-swept hills, but when you are unable to detect any obvious threat, you shrug it off and step back into the dry. Fatigue, and this strange weather, must have begun to affect your senses.

Pick a number from the *Random Number Table*. If you possess Grand Pathsmanship, for every level you have attained above the rank of Kai Grand Guardian add 1 to the number you have picked.

If your total score is now 5 or less, turn to **264**.
If it is 6 or more, turn to **125**.

## 24

You slip out of the line and enter the hut unseen. Inside you discover the following weapons:

Broadsword
Axe
Short Sword
Quiver
4 Arrows
Bow
3 Daggers
Quarterstaff

If you wish to keep any of the above, remember to make the appropriate adjustments to your *Action Chart*.

Having satisfied your curiosity, you leave the hut and rejoin the procession as it leaves the settlement.

Turn to **218**.

## 25

The brigand captain screams aloud and clutches at the fatal wound you have dealt him. His eyes glaze over and, as he falls dead at your feet, you see some of his men emerging from the surrounding pines. Rather than fight them you decide it better to escape whilst you still can and so you take to your heels, pausing only to snatch up the captain's satchel as you leave. The brigands give chase but they soon lose you among the dense pines and they give up the pursuit.

Turn to **247**.

## 26

The few acolytes who survive the combat count themselves lucky as they turn and flee for their lives. The effects of the Deathstaff upon those who fell to your blows are gruesome to look upon. Each one is drained of all blood, leaving nothing but an untidy heap of loose skin and bones. You have won the fight but not without cost. In addition to any ENDURANCE points lost during the combat, you now lose a further 5 ENDURANCE points, due to the vampirish effects of the Deathstaff.

If your ENDURANCE points total is still above 0, turn to **278**.

## 27

You let fly your shaft but it is poorly aimed. It thuds harmlessly into the window frame as the archer escapes on to the balcony.

If you wish to pursue the man, turn to **9**.
If you decide to let him go, you can leave the inn by the front door by turning to **231**.

## 28

Your refusal to pass through the arch is looked on with grave suspicion. An Elder steps forward and pushes you, telling you to affirm your vows 'like a true believer'. When you resist, he draws a dagger and curses your insubordination. Instinctively, you grab the Elder by the wrist and disarm him, but he screams in anger and Cadak responds to his cry. A gout of dark red electrical energy leaps from his staff and connects with your spine, paralysing you from neck to toe: lose 8 ENDURANCE points.

If you have survived this wounding, turn to **239**.

**29**

Gradually, the clouds knit together and shut out the sun, and once again you are plunged into the teeth of the storm. You hear a low scream carried on the wind and turn to see Cadak, blazing with anger, come striding down from his crystal dais, wielding his staff like a fiery lance. He approaches to within twenty paces and bangs the butt down twice upon the rain-drenched earth. On the second strike an umbrella of spectral light explodes overhead and falls to earth to encompass you both.

'Nothing can stop the arrival of Shamath!' screams Cadak, his eyes bright with madness. 'You have delayed her, Lone Wolf, that is all. You have not stopped her. Soon she will set foot upon the soil of Magnamund and Lord Vashna will have his revenge!'

You scan the flickering walls of this rainbow-coloured prison of light, searching for a chink in its armour through which you can escape.

'You will not escape this time,' shouts Cadak, as if he has been reading your mind. 'Not while I am alive.'

If you possess the Sommerswerd, turn to **135**.
If you wish to attack Arch Druid Cadak using the Deathstaff, turn to **213**.
If you wish to attack Cadak with a Bow and arrow, turn to **109**.
If you wish to do none of the above, turn to **252**.

### 30

You sense a hostile psychic presence about them, an evil mind-energy which is growing stronger as they draw nearer.

If you possess Kai-surge, and have reached the rank of Sun Lord or higher, turn to **229**.
If you do not possess this Discipline, or if you have yet to attain this level of Kai rank, turn to **142**.

### 31

You stand perfectly still and concentrate on attaining the trance state needed in order to effect your transition from consciousness to suspended animation. You feel as if you are drifting off to sleep, although you have entered a state in which you appear, to any outside observer, to be dead.

High above you, the unseen creature probes the fog for evidence of life force. Unable to detect any, it trails away to another part of this hellish plane in search of prey on which to feed its young. You hear

the winged beast departing and you bring yourself
out of the death-trance, awaking with a start.

Turn to **233**.

## 32

The shoreline trail winds away from Lake Vorndarol
and slowly ascends to a chalky plateau which is
covered with dense scrub. Small groups of ragged-
looking birds are perched on this foliage, feeding on
its brightly coloured blooms. As you pass by, you
reach out and grab a handful of these yellow flowers
which smell sickly-sweet.

If you wish to taste these blooms, turn to **293**.

If you decide to discard them and continue your
    ride, turn to **18**.

## 33

The alley is pitch dark but this causes you little difficulty. Using your Magnakai skill of huntmastery,
you can pick out the way ahead with ease. Your
horse is not so gifted, but he trusts to your guiding
hand to avoid the stinking debris and broken glass
which lie strewn across the cobblestones.

You are nearing a street at the alley's end when you
hear the click of a door latch. You halt, and from an
archway to your left you see two men emerge. One
is a wiry figure, partially bald; the other, a swarthy-
face villain with ragged ears and greasy blond hair.
Daggers gleam dully in their hands as they advance
towards you with murder in their eyes.

Silently you unsheathe your weapon. A few

moments later, when you re-sheathe it, it is slick with the blood of these two footpads. A search of their pockets nets you six Gold Crowns and enough food for one Meal. (Remember to adjust your *Action Chart* accordingly.)

Anxious to leave, you remount your horse and turn him to face the street at the end of the alley.

Turn to **16**.

## 34

Swiftly you sidestep the oncoming wave of automatons and leave them hacking uselessly at the air with their swords. The Demoness is putting on an armoured breastplate of varnished black steel, and she is kneeling to allow her attendants to fasten the straps. They are clumsy, and she is distracted and does not see you approaching dangerously close to the dais and the Deathstaff until it is too late. You grab the staff's cold, metallic haft and instantly you feel the terrible power that is locked within its core.

If you posses Helshezag — the sword of Darklord Kraagenskul, turn to **94**.

If you do not possess this Special Item, turn to **225**.

## 35

Bloodied and breathless from the exertion of combat, you break off the fight and take to your heels. The remaining brigands give chase, but they soon lose you among the dense pines and call off their pursuit. The area is alive with bandits and you are forced to flee northwards, away from the place where you left Bracer tethered to a tree. You are anxious for his safety and mindful that there are still many miles to be covered before you reach Lake Vorndarol, but you dare not turn back for him. Then you hear something that makes you halt in your tracks: it is the sound of a horse whinnying.

Turn to **223**.

### 36

You draw on your defensive skill of Mindblend to protect and keep hidden your psyche from the attacking horde. The vortexi are psychic creatures who actively seek out their prey by the strength of their mind waves. Your Discipline disrupts this homing process and many, in the final few hundred yards of their dive, fail to lock on to your location and waste their attack.

But there are still those among the horde who sense accurately where you are. When they attack, you are forced to defend yourself vigorously.

Vortex: COMBAT SKILL 40     ENDURANCE 22

For every level of Kai rank you have attained above that of Kai Grand Guardian, you may add 2 to your COMBAT SKILL for the duration of this fight. If you possess the Sommerswerd, add 5 to your ENDURANCE points score.

If you win the combat, turn to **46**.

### 37

In your desperation to prevent the Elder from sounding the alarm, you lash out with your clenched fist and punch him squarely on the jaw.

Pick a number from the *Random Number Table*.

If the number you have picked is *0—4*, turn to **333**.
If it is *5—9*, turn to **134**.

### 38

You survive the fall to the street without breaking any bones, but you are knocked unconscious when your head strikes the wet cobblestones. For more than an hour you lie there until you regain consciousness. Bruised, bloodied, and with a sorely aching head, you are further dismayed to discover that while you have been lying in the street, you have also been robbed.

Pick a number from the *Random Number Table* (0 = 10). The number you have picked is equal to the number of ENDURANCE points lost as a result of the fall. It is also equal to the number of Gold Crowns which have been stolen from your belt pouch, and the number of items which have gone missing from your Backpack (adjust your *Action Chart* accordingly).

Cursing your luck and the thieves of this foul city, you wearily retrace your steps back to the stables of the Crooked Sage in order to collect your horse.

Turn to **341**.

### 39

You use your Magnakai curing skills to staunch the flow of blood pouring from your gashed neck, and to mend torn muscle, but it takes several minutes before you feel the blood flow and the pain subsiding. Strength is beginning to return to your aching limbs when half a dozen loutish brigands come rushing across the rocks towards you, brandishing swords and daggers in their hands. You pull yourself wearily to your feet and unsheathe your weapon as they rush at you, stabbing and hacking with their gleaming blades.

Vakovarian brigands:
COMBAT SKILL 38     ENDURANCE 38

Due to your wound and the speed of their attack, unless you possess Grand Huntmastery you must reduce your COMBAT SKILL by 5 for the first three rounds of this combat.

You may evade combat after six rounds, by turning to **59**.

If you win the fight, turn to **348**.

### 40

You whisper the words of the Brotherhood spell 'Lightning Hand' and point at the onrushing acolytes. A tingling sensation runs down the length of your arm which culminates with a bolt of blue-white energy. It shoots from your index finger and explodes between them, killing them instantly.

Turn to **325**.

### 41

You hurry up the path and join the end of the procession. Moments later, two Elders go rushing past you on either side, screaming and cursing in an attempt to rally those acolytes who are fleeing down the track in confusion. You allow yourself a wry smile as you adjust the hood on your robe and raise your torch on high.

Turn to **250**.

## 42

You sheathe your weapon, run to the edge of the warehouse, and launch yourself towards the roof of the building opposite.

Pick a number from the *Random Number Table*. If you possess Grand Huntmastery *and* have reached the rank of Kai Grand Guardian or higher, add 3 to the number you have picked.

If your total score is now *3* or less, turn to **154**.
If it is *4–7*, turn to **310**.
If it is *8* or higher, turn to **70**.

## 43

The Elder's probe breaks through your mind shield and he suddenly realizes that you are an intruder. He pulls at your robe and tears it open, revealing your leather tunic and breeches. Recognizing them at once to be Sommlending in origin, he gasps with shock as he guesses at your true identity.

'Seize him!' he bellows, and a score of acolytes turn around and run foward to obey the command. You draw your weapon and fight them with breathtaking skill and valour, but eventually you are overcome by their numbers. By the time they have disarmed you and pinned you to the rocky ground, more than thirty of them lie slain or seriously injured in a heaped circle around where you lie.

You stare back defiantly at the ring of grim torchlit faces that loom over you. Then the face of the Elder comes into view and he sneers with disdain. He places the tip of a glowing wand to your forehead and suddenly there is an explosion of white light. Sadly for you, it is the last sensation you will ever experience.

Your life and your quest end here, on the trail to the Maakengorge.

## 44

You are standing inside a mountain of ice. A dim blue vista stretches away in every direction, and here the light appears bent and fractured by the myriad frozen facets of the water. You are encased yet you can still move; you are able to stride forwards through the seemingly solid walls as if you are moving through air.

Confidently you walk through the strange and terrible beauty of this crystal world, striding on towards the distant dim, twinkling light that first drew you to the mountains. Slowly the icy vastness begins to change and you see new wonders. There are treasures — veins of gold, raw gemstones, chests of coins, pearls, and rubies. And there are graves and lost tombs, where corpses watch your passing with burning eyes. Their ghastly stares bleed the warmth from your body and leave you shivering with psychic shock: lose 4 ENDURANCE points.

At length you pass beyond the ice and emerge into the shadowy recesses of a vast cavern. Here you discover the source of the light and in its dim glow you witness a scene that makes you tremble with fear.

Turn to **327**.

**45**
Gwynian opens his envelope and removes a time-yellowed parchment which he spreads upon the smooth stone table: it is a map of northern Magador. He points to Lake Vorndarol and tells you that the eye of the strange storms which have swept this region, has been calculated to be within a few miles of the lake's eastern shore, close to the Maakengorge. The hamlet of Vorn, or what is left of it, is located on the southern shore, near to a tributary of the River Storn. He counsels you to be on your guard at all times and, to help you succeed, he gives you an amulet of his own.

'Wear this, Grand Master,' he says, as he places the corded platinum disc around your neck. 'It will keep you safe from some of the perils that may await you at the Maakengorge.'

(Record this Platinum Amulet, which you wear on a cord around your neck, as a Special Item on your *Action Chart*. You need not discard another item in its favour if you are already carrying the maximum number permissible.)

Turn to **297**.

## 46

You have destroyed the power of the vortexi horde. They shrink and fade, and their faint, wispy remains are whipped up and dispersed by the winds of the raging storm. For a few moments there is a break in the roiling clouds and a few rays of sunlight burst through to bathe you in a warm, yellow glow. This warmth greatly invigorates your body and your mind: restore your ENDURANCE points score to its original level.

To continue, turn to **29**.

## 47

In the far corner of this hovel are a man and a woman. They are huddled close together, wide-eyed and shivering with fear. Their once-fine clothes are tattered and caked with mud, and in their midst you see that they are cradling an infant who is clearly sick with fever. You lower your weapon and offer them an assurance that you mean them no harm but, even though you can tell that they understand your words, they still look at you with terror in their eyes.

If you possess some food and wish to offer it to them, turn to **122**.

If you do not have any food, turn to **217**.

### 48

The creature roars with pain as your arrow clips its shoulder. Unfortunately, it is just a flesh wound and it does not stop the beast from advancing. You shoulder your bow and draw your weapon, bringing your horse about with your knees as you get ready to face the beast. But the instant he sees the creature, he panics and rears up on his hind legs, neighing with fright, his hooves scrabbling frantically at the air. You bring him under control using your innate Kai skills, but in doing so your attention is diverted momentarily from the attacking beast as it moves in and swipes at you with its clawed paw.

Black corvayl:
COMBAT SKILL 44     ENDURANCE 52

Reduce your COMBAT SKILL by 10 for the first round of this fight only.

If you win the combat, turn to **210**.

### 49

On closer examination you discover that one side of the amulet is covered by a detailed engraving which depicts a sinister scene. It portrays the rising up of a monstrous creature from the depths of a great gorge, flanked on all sides by a horde of skeletal warriors. At once you recognize it to be a portrayal of Darklord

III.   The creature roars with pain as your arrow clips its
shoulder.

Vashna and his minions, arising from the depths of the Maakengorge.

Turn to **238**.

### 50

The dreadful gaze of Shamath falls upon you and your blood runs cold. She points a black-gloved finger at your hiding place and speaks a thunderous phrase in the Dark Tongue that rings like metallic thunder throughout the vaulted cavern. Then, slowly, she raises her other hand and levels it beside the first. A crackling mass of electrical energy explodes into being, arcing between her outstretched palms. She flicks her massive wrists and the sparking coils of power come writhing towards you. Before you can dodge them they swirl around and encircle your body, imprisoning you in a cage of living energy.

Shamath throws back her head and the floor shudders rythmically beneath the weight of her laughter. You peer through the gaps in the swirling force field and see that her attendants are now rushing towards you.

If you possess the Dagger of Vashna, turn to **273**. If you do not possess this Special Item, turn to **179**.

### 51

You are left stunned and smouldering by the impact of the lightning ball. Drunkenly, you stagger to your feet and use your Magnakai discipline of Nexus to extinguish those parts of your cloak and tunic ignited by the blast. Then you draw the Sommerswerd and examine the hilt, but to your amazement, there is no sign of any damage whatsoever.

Your terrified horse has halted at the river's edge and you call to him, using your natural Kai skills to calm and control his fear. He responds at once and returns to collect you. Swiftly you climb back into the saddle and gallop away along the river trail, anxious to put distance between you and this deadly storm.

Turn to **80**.

## 52

Suddenly they flicker and disappear altogether from view. Frantically, you scan the brooding sky for some sign of where the creatures have gone, but it is not until you use your psychic ability that you detect them.

With your eyes closed you can picture them in your mind's eye. You see them circling their lair, then they break away and come swooping down to attack you.

You draw your weapon and detect that an aura of protection is sheathing it from the extreme temperatures of this domain. Then a hideous shriek splits the air, and you find yourself fighting the urge to open your eyes as the first of the beasts dives upon you.

Lavas: COMBAT SKILL 48     ENDURANCE 42

You may evade this combat after six rounds, by turning to **276**.

If you win the combat, turn to **3**.

## 53

'Welcome, Grand Master. I am Gwynian of Varetta,' says the grey-haired old man, in a clear voice which belies his age. 'Come and talk with me a while. Your purpose is known to me and I have something which will help your quest. Come, do not be afraid. I am a friend.'

You are shocked that he knows your true identity, but your Kai senses confirm that he is no threat to your safety. He speaks the truth.

Turn to **178**

## 54

With loathing in your heart, you advance upon your despised enemy, but he weaves his hands before his face and his image fades. He is using a spell of invisibility yet it does not keep him entirely hidden: you can still see the outline of his staff and his body flickering as he moves against the background wall of light.

Arch Druid Cadak:
COMBAT SKILL 50 ENDURANCE 35

If you win this combat, turn to **298**.

## 55

You show the runic disc and immediately the Elder's temper cools. He recognizes it to be the mark of the Guild of Rhem, the most feared brotherhood of assassins in all of northern Magnamund. He is aware that some guild assassins have been employed as agents to carry out missions for the acolytes, and he assumes at once that you are such an agent.

He backs away a few paces, bows his head, and leaves to attend to other matters at the bow of the boat. Those seated around you have now become uncomfortably curious. To avoid their attentions, you get up and move to the stern where a score of acolytes are kneeling in prayer.

Turn to **124**.

### 56

You push your way through the jostling crowd and stumble out into the street. As you turn towards the stables to go and retrieve your horse, your eagle eyes catch a glimpse of movement on a second storey balcony. It is the archer you saw a few minutes ago, the man in black who fled from the gallery.

With bated breath you watch as he climbs on to the balcony rail and leaps across the narrow street on to the roof of the building opposite.

If you possess a Bow and wish to use it, turn to **120**.

If you do not, turn to **274**.

### 57

You utter the words of the Brotherhood spell 'Net' and point your right hand at the snarling Demoness. A fluid gush of sticky strands shoot from your fingers and ensnare her legs, buying you the few precious seconds you need in order to reach the dais.

You wrench the Deathstaff from the lower tier and sag beneath its unnatural weight. In the same moment, the Demoness bursts free of the sticky net and screams with unholy anger, the noise lifting you bodily and sending you skidding across the floor.

Desperately, you fight to maintain your grip on the Deathstaff as the furious Shamath comes striding towards you. The deafening shriek of her voice rings once more in your ears as you clutch the staff to your chest and take a running leap into the dark oblivion of the shadow gate.

Turn to **270**.

## 58

You unsheathe the Sommerswerd and a halo of golden light engulfs its god-crafted blade. The dim, shadowy cavern is flooded with its goodly glow and the attendants of the Demoness Shamath waver before it. The hilt is warm in your hands and a strange feeling of miraculous ecstasy floods up your arms and courses through your body. You no longer feel as if you are wielding the sword; you are acting in concert with it. Restore 5 ENDURANCE points.

To continue, turn to **85**.

## 59

Bloodied and breathless from the exertion of combat, you break off the fight and take to your heels. The remaining brigands give chase, but they soon lose you among the boulders and undergrowth and are forced to call off their pursuit. The area is alive with bandits and you have to flee northwards, away from the copse where you left Bracer tethered. You are anxious for his safety and mindful that there are still many miles to be covered before you reach Lake

Vorndarol, but you dare not turn back for him. Then you hear something that makes you halt in your tracks: it is the sound of a horse whinnying.

Turn to **223**.

## 60

For countless minutes you hurtle into a whirling abyss of darkness and howling gales, torn by freezing winds that cut to the marrow despite your Magnakai protections. Then, as if waking from a dream, the sensation of falling abruptly ceases and you find yourself standing on a plateau of black volcanic rock, cratered and split by rivers of blazing lava. You take a tentative step forwards and feel the ground sag beneath your feet. The thin crust of cooled lava wrinkles and tears, and a jet of flickering yellow flame shoots upwards to engulf your legs.

Your Nexus skills are sufficiently developed to protect you from the flames and hellish temperature, but you are amazed that your boots and clothing have not ignited. Then you sense that your entirety is being protected by a field of energy radiating from the Platinum Amulet given you by Gwynian the Sage. Silently you thank him for his gift, for you suspect now that even your Kai skills would be hard pressed to keep you safe in this alien domain.

With difficulty you cross the semi-molten terrain and reach an island of blue-grey basalt rock, strewn with cubes of obsidian and jet. At the island's centre you discover a huge, untidy pile of cubes which make a crude temple. There is a yawning hollow at its base and, as you draw closer, you sense something is

IV.  Suddenly, a trio of horny-skinned creatures emerge
from the dark hollow.

lurking there. Suddenly, a trio of horny-skinned creatures emerge from the dark hollow and take to the air on wings that glimmer like burnished gold. You watch them ascend but you have difficulty following their flight when their bodies begin to flicker in and out of existence.

If you possess Grand Huntmastery, and have reached the rank of Sun Lord, turn to **158**.
If you do not possess this Discipline, or if you have yet to attain this level of Kai rank, turn to **52**.

## 61

Your ascent into the foothills is slowed by the difficult terrain. Thousands of huge granite boulders litter the hillside, forcing the trail to zigzag constantly on its way towards a wooded peak, less than five kilometres distant. The weather turns bitterly cold as you make the climb and, although you are protected by your innate ability of Nexus, your horse is not so fortunate. It takes you over two hours to reach the wooded peak but you are rewarded with a spectacular view of Lake Vorndarol.

The descent from the peak is far easier. The trail is wide and less tortuous, and the peak itself protects you and your horse from the icy winds that are blowing in off the lake. You have gone a little over a kilometre when suddenly your pathsmanship skills alert you to danger; you sense that there is an ambush ahead. You turn off the trail and dismount, leaving your horse tied to a boulder, while you scout the way ahead on foot. You draw your weapon and keep it to hand in case you should happen once more upon some skulking brigands.

Soon you arrive at a granite outcrop which overlooks a small clearing among the boulders below. In the centre of this clearing lies the carcass of a wild boar.

If you wish to descend to the clearing and examine the carcass more closely, turn to **17**.

If you would rather wait here and observe the clearing from a distance, turn to **88**.

### 62

The fat drunkard can hardly believe his luck when you reach to your belt pouch and count out ten Gold Crowns into his grubby hand.

'May the gods bless y' boots, sir!' he cackles, as he stuffs the gleaming crowns into his pocket. 'If it's the Crooked Sage you be a'wantin' to visit, you be needin' Tavern Lane, o'er there,' he says, enthusiastically pointing to the street which leads off to the east.

With the drunkard's gleeful laughter echoing in your ears, you spur Bracer to a canter and enter this foul-smelling street. Clamped against the walls of the surrounding buildings are oil-soaked torches which serve to illuminate the signs of wine shops and taverns. They are crudely painted with emblems — a bloodied battle-axe, a winged horse, a watery sun rising from a broken skull. There is not one which resembles a crooked sage and you are beginning to suspect you have been duped, when suddenly you hear the sound of drunken revelry coming from a two-storey building at the end of the street. Its oaken doors hang open and the vivid orange glare of its roaring hearth spills invitingly into the dank night gloom. Although it has no painted emblem, you sense at once that you have come to the Crooked Sage Inn.

At your approach, a sallow-faced stable boy limps from a wooden hut which is leaning precariously against the side of the tavern wall. For a Gold Crown (erase this from your *Action Chart*), he takes charge of your horse and shows you to the taproom door.

Turn to **21**.

**63**

You look towards the dais and see a staff of twisted black metal. Its two metre length looks insignificant lying beside the huge, booted foot of the Demoness.

'The time has nearly come for the transference,' says the young woman. 'Shamath must be stopped, and only you can stop her.'

'But how?' you reply, bemused.

'Simple! You must steal the Deathstaff and enter the shadow gate before her. Use the staff to destroy Cadak's crystal dais — this will close the gate and prevent the Demoness from entering Magnamund. But I warn you, Lone Wolf. You will have precious little time to accomplish this, so do not delay once you return to your world. You must destroy Cadak's dais as quickly as possible or Shamath will get through. She has great strength and power here, but on Magnamund her powers would make her invincible.'

The young woman looks over her shoulder, as if she is being pursued by some invisible hunter. 'I wish I could help you more, Lone Wolf,' she says, anxiously, 'but I have my own battle to fight. Be brave, Grand Master, but most of all — be swift!'

And with these words she begins to fade before your eyes. The moment she vanishes completely, the cavern echoes to a deafening roar. It is the angry cry of Shamath. She has seen you!

Turn to **50**.

**64**

You strike camp and set off shortly after dawn. Come mid-morning, you arrive at a high pass from where you see Lake Vorndarol for the first time. You call on your Magnakai skill of huntmastery to intensify your vision and, as your view of the lake grows sharper and clearer, you make out the ruins of Vorn on the southern shore. The hamlet is blackened and desolate but it is not without signs of life. There are men moving around in the streets and a square-rigged boat is moored at the quay.

Bayan is anxious for his family's safety and keen to return to them now that he has guided you to within sight of Vorn. You thank him for his help and offer him some money which he gratefully accepts. Pick a number from the *Random Number Table* (0 = 10). The number you have chosen is equal to the number of Gold Crowns you give to Bayan. If you have insufficient money, you must give him all the Gold Crowns you have, plus an item from your Backpack.

To continue, turn to **8**.

# 65

The howling phantoms come swirling out of the storm. They encircle the great shimmering arch in a long, unbroken chain, and then, one by one, they peel away to dive at the place where you are standing.

Your Kai instincts inform you that the Deathstaff possesses the power to repel these psychic phantoms, if you have the courage to use it. You also sense that there will inevitably be a price to pay if you use a weapon forged by the King of all Darkness.

If you wish to use the Deathstaff, turn to **263**.
If you decide not to use this weapon, turn to **83**.

# 66

You awake shortly after dawn to the smell of freshly-brewed jala. Fyrad has already risen and is busy preparing breakfast. He hands you a steaming mug and you look out over the damp hillside, contemplating the quest whilst sipping this delicious beverage.

After breakfast, Fyrad tells you of a pass which leads directly to the east shore, then he gathers his equipment and furs and loads them on to his mule. He is tired of dodging brigands and storms and has decided to strike camp and abandon his hunt in the mountains. You bid each other good luck before saying your final farewells. On leaving the cave, you turn to the east and Fyrad to the south.

The hunter's directions are accurate and useful. You find the pass and by noon you have reached a chalky plateau on the far side, which is covered with dense scrub. Small groups of ragged-looking birds are perched on this foliage, feeding on its brightly coloured blooms. As you pass by, you reach out and grab a handful of these yellow flowers which smell sickly-sweet.

If you wish to taste these blooms, turn to **293**.
If you decide to discard them and continue your ride, turn to **18**.

The muddy track climbs to the peak of a ridge and then makes a twisting descent to a copse of sickly-looking trees clustered at the base of a gulley. You have noticed that the night wind has gradually been getting warmer and, as you reach the copse, a few drops of rain begin to spatter the shoulders of your cloak. Within minutes this gentle shower is transformed into a torrential downpour. Suddenly, thunder booms overhead and forks of white lightning streak down to explode among the surrounding trees, setting them on fire. Fearful of the danger, you peer through the wall of rain in search of safer shelter.

Aided by your Kai senses, you detect two possible refuges from the storm: an overhanging ledge of rock, and the entrance to an old mineshaft.

If you wish to take shelter under the ledge, turn to **209**.

If you decide to seek shelter in the old mineshaft turn to **128**.

### 68

The unexpected sight of your dead brother's face leaves you dry-mouthed and shaking, but fortunately your Kai mastery of psychic defence protects your mind from the full effects of this psychic shock: lose 2 ENDURANCE points.

Turn to **195**.

### 69

Instinctively, you dodge your head to one side to avoid being hit in the face by this deadly missile.

Pick a number from the *Random Number Table*. If you possess Grand Huntmastery, add 2 to the number you have picked.

If your total score is now 3 or less, turn to **271**.

If it is 4 or more, turn to **165**.

### 70

You make the jump look effortless as you glide through the air and make a perfect landing on the opposite roof. For a moment the black-clad archer halts beside a tall chimney stack and turns around to look at you. He is clearly worried by how efficiently you are pursuing him. Then, three other shadowy figures emerge from behind the stack and stand at his shoulder. Silently they stare at you for a few moments before one of their number raises his hand and hurls a glassy sphere in your direction.

The sphere shatters at your feet and, in an instant, your legs are engulfed by a writhing mass of magical vines. By the time you have freed yourself, you discover that the assassin and his confederates are nowhere to be seen. Cautiously, you approach the chimney stack where you find, lying at its base, a palm-sized coin of black metal engraved with runes. You pick up this disc and slip it into the pocket of your tunic. (Record this Runic Disc on you *Action Chart* as a Special Item. You must discard an item in its favour if you already carry the maximum number permissible.)

Having lost sight of the four shadowy figures, you decide now to call off the chase. Wearily you make your way down from the roof and retrace your steps back to the stables of the Crooked Sage in order to collect your horse.

Turn to **341**.

Hurriedly, you recite the words that trigger the Brotherhood spell 'Counterspell'. To your sudden horror you discover that the spell is ineffective against this energy bolt and, with a blinding eruption of white light, it explodes among the charred timbers. The blast and concussion send you reeling backwards to slam against a soot-blackened wall: lose 12 ENDURANCE points.

If you are still alive, turn to **200**.

## 72

The umbrella of light quickly fades to leave you standing in a torrential rain-storm, close to the base of the crystal dais. Through the downpour you can see that the acolytes are slowly returning. They are anxious for the safety of their leader and hungry for the successful summonation of their banished lord.

Despite the chill, you tighten your grip on the icy-cold Deathstaff and climb the tiers to the top of the dais. You sense that the crystal dais commands the opening and closing of the shadow gate and you know you must try to close the gate before Shamath appears. In frustration, you raise the Deathstaff and bring it crashing down upon the floor of the upper tier, but it does little damage. It could take forever to destroy the dais this way.

Then a wave of electrical energy crackles around the rim of the great arch and your blood runs cold, for you know that in a dim and distant cavern upon the plane of Darkness, the Demoness Shamath has just stepped into a shadow gate. Her journey to Magnamund has begun!

Turn to **164**.

## 73

You dig your heels into Bracer's flanks to make him gallop along the track, away from the rocky ledge and the onrushing wall of water which threatens to drown you both. Unfortunately, you have covered no further than a few dozen metres when you are caught and overrun by the raging flood.

For countless minutes you hurtle along the gulley, propelled by the torrential flood waters. Your terrifying experience comes to an end when you are deposited on a tiny island of rock in the centre of the raging flow. A few minutes later you catch sight of Bracer; he is standing on a ridge of high ground near the edge of the gulley. He is clearly frightened but he looks to be physically unharmed by his ordeal. You spend a long and miserable night on this rock, waiting for the flood waters to subside. Due to injuries sustained in the flood you lose 5 ENDURANCE points.

Turn to **12**.

**74**

You draw on your Magnakai Discipline of Psi-screen to keep safe your identity from the Elder's mind probe. You sense that his psychic power is strong and you fear that your defences may not be sufficient to repel him.

Pick a number from the *Random Number Table*. If you possess Assimilance, add 3 to the number you have picked. Also, if you possess Grand Nexus, add 3; and if you possess Kai-alchemy, add 2.

If your total score is now 9 or less, turn to **43**.
If it is 10 or more, turn to **258**.

## 75

You hold the brigand in a vice-tight arm lock and demand to know who sent him here to ambush you.

'No one sent me,' he pleads, 'no one . . . no one at all. I was plannin' on robbin' me a few acolytes, that's all. Some of 'em has gold and trinkets that's worth cash in Vakovar. This trail's been good to me. It's netted me some rich pickin's in the past month or so. We wern't after you in partic'lar . . . no, you jus' happened to come ridin' past, that's all.'

Your Kai senses inform you that he is speaking the truth. He and his band of robbers have been waylaying acolytes of Vashna who have travelled this route over the past few weeks. Without slackening your grip, you ask him what he knows about them.

'They been preparin' something, over on the . . .' he says, but he ceases to speak the moment he sees a group of his men emerge from the surrounding pines.

'You're in for it now,' he hisses, 'my men are goin' to do for you good an' proper.'

Another six of the captain's men step from out of the trees and begin to move towards you, their swords held ready to strike. Rather than stay and fight them, you shove the captain away and take to your heels, pausing only to snatch up his satchel as you make your escape.

Screaming curses and promising you a slow death, the captain scrambles to his feet and leads his men in a chase, but you are soon lost among the dense pines and, reluctantly, he orders his henchmen to give up the pursuit.

Turn to **247**.

You don a red robe, taken from one of the dead acolytes, and raise its black hood to keep your face hidden. The folds of this voluminous garment cover your weapons as well as your clothing, and a haversack taken from another acolyte battle-corpse is large enough to conceal your Backpack. Confident that you can pass for one of them, you run to the quayside and join with those acolytes who are now climbing aboard the longboat.

When your turn comes, you leap from the quay on to the deck of the ship. You land very close to the sandalled feet of one of the three acolyte Elders and he glares at you angrily, though he does not see through your disguise. You take your place on a bench alongside the others and use your Kai camouflage skills to avoid their attention. You notice that a bank of oars stands upright in the gunwales of the boat, and it strikes you as odd that no order has been given to man them. When the last of the acolytes are safely aboard, you discover why.

Turn to **93**.

## 77

You leave the furrier's shop and remount your horse to continue your search for the Crooked Sage Inn. You have ridden less than twenty metres when a sudden gust of wind thins out the cloying fog, revealing the dark entrance to an alleyway off to your right.

If you wish to explore this alley, turn to **33**.

If you decide to ignore it and continue on your way along this street, turn to **147**.

## 78

Drawing on your mastery of psychic defence, you are able to construct a fortress wall around your mind which absorbs the Elder's probe. He learns nothing from his attempt to read your psyche and, rather than admit to failure, he dismisses you as an empty-headed cretin.

With a growl of disdain, he orders you to rejoin the procession and pushes you out of his way as he strides back to his position beside the altar.

Turn to **250**.

## 79

As you slay the last of the ghastly spawn, you feel the floor beginning to harden. Hurriedly, you stretch out and grab the rough cavern wall and pull your feet free before the floor sets and you are held fast forever.

The automatons have ceased to move. They stand like frozen statues in a line across the cavern. You seize your chance and race towards the dais, but the Demoness is watching you and now she is aware of your plan. She has no intention of allowing you anywhere near the dais or the Deathstaff.

If you possess Kai-alchemy, turn to **57**.
If you do not possess this Grand Master Discipline, turn to **282**.

## 80

The rumble and crack of repeated lightning ball strikes echo in your wake as you make your hurried escape along the river trail. It is not until you traverse a high pass, where the River Storn flows through the mountain foothills, that the sound eventually disappears. Your senses tingle with the conviction that the storm was no accident; you feel sure that a malevolent elemental force is at work here.

Shortly before dusk, you emerge from the pass and see Lake Vorndarol for the first time. You call on your Magnakai skill of huntmastery to intensify your vision and, as your view of the lake grows sharper and clearer, you make out the ruins of Vorn on the southern shore. The hamlet is blackened and desolate but it is not without signs of life. There are several pinpoints of light, camp fires judging by their colour, and you can see a square-rigged mainsail: there is a boat moored at the quay.

If you wish to attempt to reach Vorn before nightfall, turn to **203**.

If you decide to try to spend the night in the hills and then approach the hamlet in the morning, turn to **117**.

## 81

The instant you step through the archway you feel an electrifying jolt run through your body, and a writhing snake of blue-white energy arcs from the rim of the arch to the hilt of the sword Helshezag. A gasp of astonishment arises from the acolytes, audible even above the howling wind.

'We have an intruder in our midst,' screams Cadak, levelling his wizard's staff at you accusingly. You fight the paralysing effect of the current and tug the sword free of its scabbard. For a moment the current weakens as it is absorbed and neutralized by the dark energy of Helshezag, but then the tip of Cadak's staff ignites with a crimson flame and the current intensifies anew, numbing your limbs with its insidious effect.

Turn to **228**.

## 82

The Elder becomes angry. He scolds you for taking a 'forbidden' weapon and he orders you to hand it over to him at once. Aware that most of the acolytes in this section of the boat are watching you, and that any resistance would be sure to lead to the revealing of your true identity, you reach inside your robe and undo the buckle of your weapon's belt. It clatters to the deck and the Elder snatches it up and hurls it into the lake. (Erase from your *Weapons List* any hand weapons you possess. If you have a Bow, you may still keep it.)

Still fuming, the Elder orders you to go to the rear of the ship where a score of acolytes are kneeling in prayer, and plead to the spirit of Vashna for forgiveness.

Turn to **124**.

## 83

You resist the urge to make use of the Deathstaff to ward off the approaching vortexi horde. You would rather trust in your own goodly powers than use a weapon forged of evil.

Lashed by the wind and the rain, you steel yourself as the screaming phantoms come swooping down to attack.

If you possess Assimilance, and have attained the rank of Kai Grand Guardian, turn to **103**.

If you possess Kai-screen, and have attained the rank of Kai Grand Guardian, turn to **36**.

If you do not possess these skills, or if you have yet to attain this level of Kai mastery, turn to **144**.

## 84

'Do you mind if I keep this?' you ask, motioning to the amulet.

'I've no objection,' replies Kadharian. 'I hope it helps you to discover what is truly going on in the north.'

Carefully you rewrap the talisman and slip it into the pocket of your tunic (record this Black Talisman as a Special Item on your *Action Chart* — you need not discard another item in its favour if you already possess the maximum allowed). Then, after a meal

V.  A dishevelled fat man with a yellow streaked beard.

and a soothingly hot bath, you bid farewell to the President and take your leave of the palace by way of the stables.

Night has thickened the blanket of mist which lines the narrow streets and alleys of Helgor. Guided by your Kai instincts, you set off northwards, but soon you have cause to regret not having thought of asking Kadharian for directions to the Crooked Sage Inn. Helgor is an old city and its chaotic streets follow no logical plan. After several wrong turns you come upon a square where the vanes of a rotting signpost point to three exits. Slumped at its base there sits a dishevelled fat man with a yellow streaked beard, who is gulping mouthfuls of cheap ale from a filthy stone pitcher. You attempt to use your Kai paths-manship skill to read the signpost but with no success — it is completely illegible.

If you wish to leave the square by the north exit, turn to **16**.

If you wish to leave the square by the east exit, turn to **332**.

If you wish to leave the square by the west exit, turn to **161**.

If you decide to ask the fat man for directions to the Crooked Sage Inn, turn to **287**.

### 85

At Shamath's command, the attendants draw slivers of steel and come rushing to hack you down. You essay a wide sweep of the sword and scythe the front rank down as easily as if they were ripened corn. Your sword strokes feel effortless; it is as if you are merely holding the Sommerswerd and the blade itself is fighting of its own accord. Within the space of a few minutes you have slain every last one of Shamath's attendants, over a hundred in number.

Turn to **242**.

**86**

Using the Brotherhood spell 'Sense Evil' you determine that the token is a cursed relic which has been activated by its proximity to the pool of stagnant water. The closer you get to the pool, the hotter the relic becomes. Another few steps and it will explode. Desperately, you fumble to retrieve it from the smoking pocket of your tunic, and hurl it away.

Pick a number from the *Random Number Table*.

If the number you have picked is 0–3, turn to **96**.
If it is 4–9, turn to **316**.

**87**

You are nearing the middle of the river when your acute hearing detects the cawing of birds in the far distance. At first you dismiss the sounds, thinking they are probably birds of prey feeding somewhere high in the mountains, but when the cawing rapidly grows louder you look upwards to try to detect where it is coming from. You do not have to look very far.

Three hundred metres above you, a flock of ugly black birds are cawing excitedly as they ride a thermal air current. You recognize them to be Durncrag scavengers, cruel predators native only to these mountains. Then, with an awful suddenness, they come diving towards you, screeching like demons as they prepare to strike with beak and claw.

If you possess Animal Mastery and have reached the rank of Sun Knight or higher, turn to **249**.

If you do not possess this Discipline, or if you have yet to attain this level of Grand Mastery, turn to **180**.

## 88

For half an hour you crouch among the boulders, your eyes scanning every inch of the terrain which surrounds the clearing, but you detect nothing untoward. Then the silence is broken by a sharp *clack!* and a small rock comes tumbling down the slope. You catch sight of movement among some bushes at the top of the slope, and you sense at once that someone is hiding there.

If you possess a Bow and wish to fire an arrow into the bushes, turn to **227**.

If you do not, turn to **320**.

## 89

You utilize your powers to subdue the growling wolf and immediately he becomes calm and docile. Within a few minutes you exact a transformation that turns this creature from a wild animal into a loyal and friendly ally.

While you settle down to rest, the wolf watches over you and Bracer, attentively standing guard at the entrance to the mineshaft.

Restore 3 ENDURANCE points and turn to **279**.

## 90

The great winged beast ekes out its death throes for several minutes after you strike the fatal blow. Aching with the fatigue of your combat, you stagger away from its carcass and stumble blindly through the fog. Soon you sense the temperature beginning to drop and the great grey wall of fog gradually condenses and falls as rain. This rain freezes and you quickly find yourself surrounded by a wall of glittering ice which stretches like a range of jagged glass mountains from horizon to horizon.

Turn to **187**.

## 91

The hollow is damp and draughty and offers poor protection against the elements. There is little foliage on which to feed your mount and the incessant storm winds howl through the gaps in the rocks, making it impossible for you to sleep.

During this long and uncomfortable night, unless you possess Grand Huntmastery you must eat a Meal or lose 3 ENDURANCE points.

Shortly before dawn the storm dies down and you are able to snatch an hour's sleep. Unfortunately, it is insufficient rest to refresh you fully: lose 3 ENDURANCE points.

To continue, turn to **285**.

## 92

One of the bolts hits your Backpack (erase 2 items from your Backpack List) but you manage to stay on your feet and reach the dais. You wrench the

Deathstaff from the floor of the lower tier and sag beneath its unnatural weight. The Demoness spins around and emits a terrible scream when she sees what you are holding. The noise of her wrath lifts you bodily and sends you skidding helplessly across the floor.

Desperately, you fight to maintain your grip on the Deathstaff as the furious Shamath comes striding towards you. The deafening shriek of her voice rings once more in your ears as you clutch the Deathstaff to your chest and take a running leap into the dark oblivion of the shadow gate.

Turn to **270**.

With the returning acolytes aboard, an Elder gives the order that the grappling lines and planks – which hold the longboat secure to the Vakovarian ship – be cut and tossed into the lake. The moment this is done, the three Elders raise their glowing wands of power and touch them together to form a triangle. There is a flash of greenish light and a swirling cone of vapour coils into the sky, pouring from the tip of this triangle. It creates a howling wind which fills the sails and catapults the longboat away from the quayside at tremendous speed. It takes just a few minutes for the ruins of Vorn to disappear over the horizon.

Aboard the longboat the victorious acolytes busy themselves as the cold waters of Lake Vorndarol speed by beneath the keel. Some are attending to those who were wounded in the battle; others are chanting a sombre dirge or sitting quietly with their heads bowed, lost in unholy prayer; the remainder clean their weapons or stare vacantly at the distant mountains.

You keep your head bowed and pretend to be praying. The deception seems to be working until a hand suddenly grips your shoulder and you hear a gruff voice bark a command in a language you do not readily understand.

If you possess Grand Pathsmanship, turn to **243**.
If you do not possess this Discipline, turn to **184**.

### 94

There is a thunderous *Crack!* as a bolt of white lightning leaps from the Deathstaff and connects with the hilt of Helshezag. You feel an agonizing pain wrack your body from skull to toe: lose 5 ENDURANCE points. Then, with a breathtaking suddenness, the pain ceases.

You open your eyes and look down, and to your astonishment you see the scorched remains of Helshezag lying at the foot of the dais, the sword obliterated by the power of the Deathstaff (erase Helshezag from your Special Items list).

To continue, turn to **318**.

### 95

You are nearing the top of the steps when three shadowy figures emerge from behind a chimney stack and block your path to the approaching archer. One of them has something in his hand which he hurls in your direction: it is a small glass sphere.

The sphere shatters upon the iron steps and, in an instant, your feet and legs are engulfed by a writhing mass of magical vines. By the time you have freed yourself from their vice-like grip, you discover that the archer and his confederates are nowhere to be seen. Having lost sight of the four shadowy figures, you decide to call off the chase. Wearily you make your way down from the roof and retrace your steps back to the stables of the Crooked Sage in order to collect your horse.

Turn to **341**.

**96**

You throw the red-hot token away, but it hits a boulder and rebounds directly into the trough. There is a dreadful moment of silence, then the whole area is lit up by a blinding flash of yellow flame and suddenly everything seems to be happening in slow motion. You see acolytes tumbling backwards, screaming, their robes sprouting tongues of flame, and chunks of marble from the trough hurtling skywards like fiery meteors. Then the heat and the shock of the explosion rips into your face and chest, sending you cartwheeling backwards into a black, unfeeling oblivion.

Tragically, your life and your quest end here, on the trail to the Maakengorge.

**97**

At Shamath's command, the attendants draw vicious-looking slivers of steel from scabbards hidden inside their robes, and come rushing forwards to hack you down.

VI.    The attendants draw viscious-looking slivers of steel
       from scabbards hidden inside their robes.

Cheghath: COMBAT SKILL 37    ENDURANCE 40

These beings are gifted with strong psychic defences. Halve all bonuses you would normally receive if you choose to use a psychic attack (including Kai Blast) during this combat.

If you win the combat, turn to **303**.

## 98

After a few minutes it is clear that the brigands have no idea where you are. The leader is furious; he turns to his henchmen and orders them to find you at once. One by one his brutish sidekicks scurry away into the surrounding trees until the leader is left all alone.

If you wish to launch a surprise attack on the brigand leader, turn to **14**.

If you wish to creep forward and attempt to take him hostage, turn to **291**.

## 99

The jackals are gaining too quickly for you to outrun them; your only hope now is to fight them off. You rein your exhausted horse to a halt and slip out of the saddle, drawing your weapon as you touch the ground. The jackals spread out and surround you, howling maniacally as they savour the scent of your frightened horse. Then, as if responding to a silent signal, they slink forward to tighten the circle.

Your horse rears up and tries to pull away, his hooves flailing the air perilously close to your skull. As the first of the jackals makes its attack, you find yourself struggling to hold on to the reins with one hand and fight the jackals off with the other.

Vorndarol jackals:
COMBAT SKILL 42    ENDURANCE 38

Unless you possess Grand Weaponmastery and have reached the rank of Sun Knight, or higher, you must reduce your COMBAT SKILL by 5 for the duration of this combat.

>    You may evade combat after four rounds, by turning to **222**.
>    If you win this fight, turn to **347**.

**100**

You follow the President into the chamber, your footsteps echoing as you walk across the mosaic marble floor. At the far end of the room a wiry wolfhound lies snoozing in front of a log fire which is crackling in an iron grate. The flames illuminate the chamber with a warm glow, casting flickering shadows across countless shelves stacked with thick rolls of parchment and papyrus. At the centre there stands a large table heaped with sand. The sand has been shaped to depict the topography of Magador, its towns, cities, mountains, hills and rivers. The attention to detail is most impressive.

'Somewhere, here, I fear there is a great evil at work,' says Kadharian, pointing to a section of the table which depicts the territory north of Lake Vorndarol, an area uncomfortably close to the deep furrow which represents the Maakengorge.

'Three moons ago, the lakeside hamlet of Vorn was reportedly destroyed by an unnatural storm, the first of many that have continuously swept the region. I dispatched a troop of my guards to investigate but they never returned. Since then, a second troop has also disappeared without trace.'

'But what makes you think that a plot to resurrect Vashna is afoot?' you reply, trying not to sound overly sceptical. 'With due respect, President, this is a notorious region infested with renegades and brigands. There may be a far simpler explanation for the destruction of Vorn and the disappearance of your troops.'

'Aye, t'is so,' retorts Kadharian. 'At first I, too, made the same assumption. But then I came into the possession of something which made me believe otherwise.'

From a leather pouch hanging from his sword belt, Kadharian takes an item which is neatly wrapped in a square of patterned silk.

'Here, Grand Master,' he says, offering it to you, 'I'll let you draw your own conclusions from this.'

Turn to **133**.

## 101

You are so stunned by the image of your dead brother's face that your mind enters a deep state of psychic shock: lose 8 ENDURANCE points.

If you survive the effects of this trauma, turn to **195**.

## 102

You sense that you are not alone; you can feel the

presence of another living creature close by. Silently you draw your weapon and set off on foot to investigate and your Kai senses lead you directly to a derelict hut on the perimeter of this ancient settlement. You call out, demanding whoever is inside to show himself, but there is no reply. You repeat your demand but again it goes unanswered. With weapon raised you rush in through the door, expecting to have to fight a skulking brigand or an acolyte of Vashna, but you find neither. You are confronted instead by something wholly unexpected.

Turn to **47**.

**103**

You draw on your Kai mastery to conjure up a dense fog to surround you, in the hope that it will hamper the attacking horde. However, the vortexi are psychic creatures who actively seek out their prey by the strength of their mind waves. Your Discipline disrupts this homing process to some extent, but there are still many among the phantom horde who sense accurately where you are. When they attack, you are forced to defend yourself vigorously.

Vortexi: COMBAT SKILL 44    ENDURANCE 30

For every level of Kai rank you have attained above that of Kai Grand Guardian, you may add 2 to your COMBAT SKILL for the duration of this fight. If you possess the Sommerswerd, add 5 to your ENDURANCE points score.

If you win the combat, turn to **46**.

## 104

You dig your heels into Bracer's flanks and gallop along the track, steering him away from the rocky ledge and the onrushing wall of water which threatens to drown you both. Helped by your Kai mastery, you make him leave the track and ascend a difficult slope that leads to higher ground. He obeys your command and, with barely seconds to spare, you avoid being caught by the flood as it careers along the gulley.

The remaining few hours before sunrise are spent on a tiny island of rock, waiting for the flood waters to subside. It is a long and uncomfortable wait: lose 2 ENDURANCE points.

Turn to **12**.

## 105

The journey to Helgor takes you south to the Citystate of Casiorn, then west to the Lyrisian capital of Varetta – a road you once travelled several years ago during your Magnakai quest. In the main, your ride is peaceably uneventful. By choice you keep to yourself and avoid staying too long in any one place. It is not until you reach Vakovar that the uncertain politics of this region give rise for concern. This squalid, lawless city is home to some of the Stornlands' most notorious criminals and robber-barons. It is common knowledge that travellers who value their wealth and health wisely avoid Vakovar whenever possible. Forewarned by these rumours you choose not to dwell here, but ride swiftly through the city and press on to Helgor. Yet while you are within the city walls of Vakovar no less than a dozen separate attempts are made to relieve you of your money pouch and horse. There are no witnesses to these attacks, which is just as well, for when you ride out of Vakovar you leave a score of dead robbers littering the cobblestones.

It is early evening when you eventually crest a hill and catch your first disappointing glimpse of Helgor. It is a damp and unwholesome-looking city, ringed by a rampart of mouldering rubble, the remains of a curtain wall which was destoyed during the war against the Darklords. Through the many gaps in this rampart you can see the thick fog that swirls through Helgor's brick streets and crooked, filthy alleys. At first sight it seems that the Magadorian capital is little more than a beggar-city, a vast hotchpotch of slums and hovels, but as you ride nearer you notice several grand towers piercing the rolling grey mist.

The main approach to Helgor is patrolled by presidential guards, heavily armed with crossbows and spears, who are checking everyone attempting to enter by road. They are dressed in flamboyant tunics of green, scarlet, and black calf hide, which seem too lavish for the garrison of such a squalid city. When asked your business, you show them the scroll given to you by Rimoah. They are impressed by the invitation and insist that an armed escort be provided to take you directly to the President's palace. After your experience at Vakovar you welcome their offer.

Despite the overwhelming squalor of Helgor's dingy tenements and streets, you were expecting the President's palace to be the exception. To your disappointment, it turns out to be little more than a fortified chateau situated at the centre of the city, atop a hill known as the Vanagrom Knoll. You are welcomed into the palace's senate hall by an official called Stepona, a dour man who looks older than his thirty years. He sees to it that your horse is stabled, and that you are given refreshments while you await your audience with the President. An hour passes before the doors to the senate hall swing open and, without formal announcement, in strides President Kadharian of Magador.

If you have ever visited the city of Aarnak in a previous Lone Wolf adventure, turn to **315**.

If you have never been to Aarnak, turn to **202**.

## 106

You draw on your psychic defences to keep you hidden from this creature. You cannot see it in the dense fog but you can hear it swooping down, and you are nearly flattened by the draught of its mighty wings as it roars past close overhead.

As first it seems to be going away into the distance, but then you sense it turn about and come gliding back for a second pass. Suddenly you realize that your psychic defences are not hiding you from this creature at all; it is locking on to your life force, not your mind.

If you have a Bow and wish to use it, turn to **254**.

If you do not possess this weapon, or do not wish to use it, turn to **152**.

### 107

You recite the words of the battle spell 'Invisible Fist' and suddenly you feel a powerful gust of wind sweep past your face. It punches the Elder squarely in the stomach, lifts him off his feet, and sends him tumbling over the side of the boat.

A cry goes up along the deck, a shout of alarm that

one of the Elders has fallen overboard. Scores of acolytes rush to the rail in response but there is nothing they can do. The longboat is travelling so fast that the Elder is already hundreds of metres behind the stern and cannot be seen amidst the churning water.

Those who were seated near you have now become uncomfortably curious about who you are. To avoid their attentions, you move to the stern where a score of acolytes are kneeling in prayer.

Turn to **124**.

## 108

'Calm yourself, Smudd,' you say, purposefully letting your hands drift away from your weapons, 'I mean you no harm. I just want to talk with you awhile, that's all.'

The scrawny-faced knave stares at you with deep suspicion. Cold sweat beads upon his brow and his hand tightens on the hilt of his rapier.

'Look,' you say, reaching to your Backpack, 'I'm even prepared to compensate you for the privilege.'

Slowly you unshoulder your Backpack, unbuckle the flap, and offer him any item of his choosing. After some hesitation he picks the item which is listed at the top of your Backpack List. (Erase this item from your *Action Chart*.)

To continue, turn to **323**.

## 109

You raise your bow and draw an arrow, but the

instant the feathers touch your lips, both the bow and the arrow burst into flames: lose 2 ENDURANCE points.

Cadak cackles with glee at the success of his spell. 'You are doomed, Lone Wolf. Why don't you admit it,' he says, sneeringly. 'You were doomed the moment you returned from the great arch.'

Turn to **252**.

### 110

The instant you correctly complete the second sequence, a deep hum resonates from inside the upper tier and slowly it opens to reveal a hexagonal crystal plinth with a circular hole at its centre. Your Kai senses inform you that by inserting the tip of the Deathstaff into the hole, you will cause the shadow gate beneath the great arch to close.

Trembling with fear and exhilaration, you raise the Deathstaff above your head and bring it down with one mighty thrust, driving it deep into the hole.

Turn to **246**.

### 111

You sense a hostile psychic presence about them, an evil mind-energy which is becoming stronger as they draw nearer. You draw on your own formidable psychic skills and erect a defensive wall around your mind which keeps you safe from their first bombardment. They veer upwards and vanish into the clouds for a few moments, but then they reappear and come swooping down for another attack.

If you possess Kai-surge, and have reached the rank of Sun Lord, or higher, turn to **229**.

If you do not possess this Discipline, of if you have yet to attain this level of Kai rank, turn to **142**.

## 112

Using your Kai mastery, you steer your exhausted horse across this difficult terrain with incredible skill. You manage to keep him ahead of the jackals just long enough to reach firmer ground, where he is then able to increase his pace and escape from the howling pack.

The jackals command the shore and you are forced to retrace your steps all the way back to the fork in the trail and take the other path that leads into the foothills. By the time you arrive here, you are tired and very hungry. Unless you possess Grand Hunt-mastery, you must eat 2 meals or lose 6 ENDURANCE points.

To continue, turn to **61**.

## 113

You stretch out with your right foot and kick open the satchel, but in doing so you place yourself off-balance. The brigand captain senses this and uses the opportunity to break free. He scurries away for the safety of the trees, screaming all the while for his men to come and save him. Then you see the first of them emerging from the surrounding pines. Rather than fight them you decide it better to escape whilst you still can and so you take to your heels, pausing only to snatch up the captain's satchel as you leave. The brigands give chase but they soon lose you among the dense pines and call off their pursuit.

Turn to **247**.

## 114

You recover quickly from the unexpected shock and manage to keep your place in the line as it moves up the hillside, away from the poisoned trough, without displaying any discomfort.

Turn to **250**.

## 115

You command her to raise her right hand and she does so without hesitation. On her index finger you notice a platinum ring which you sense at once is magical; it is the source of her psychic power. The ring is fused to her hand and cannot be removed. Having no wish to sever her finger, you command her to lower her hand and tell you where you may find the Crooked Sage Inn. Obediently, she gives you clear directions to Tavern Lane, the street where the inn is situated, and less than ten minutes later you find yourself at a signpost which marks the entrance to this narrow thoroughfare.

Turn to **332**.

### 116

The Elder scolds you for more than a minute before he loses his patience and stalks off, dismissing you as unworthy of his time. Those seated around you have now become uncomfortably curious about who you are. To avoid their attentions, you get up and move to the stern where a score of acolytes are kneeling in prayer.

Turn to **124**.

### 117

You find shelter in a wooded grove, close to the trail, where you are able to make camp for the night. Darkness descends, but the surrounding trees are kept illuminated by a spectacular host of twinkling lights which swoop and soar above the hills. It is a wondrous display but you are not deceived into thinking that all is well. There is a great and evil magic at work here; you can sense it.

The storms stay away this night and you are able to get several hours' uninterrupted sleep — restore 3 ENDURANCE points. You rise with the dawn and breakfast on roots and berries which are in plentiful supply (there is sufficient surplus for 2 Meals). Then you break camp and continue your ride towards Vorn.

Turn to **8**.

### 118

You raise the sun-sword and strike out with unerring accuracy as the first of the Vortexi engulf you.

Vortexi: COMBAT SKILL 49    ENDURANCE 48

For possessing the Sommerswerd, add 5 to your ENDURANCE points score. For every level of Kai rank you have attained above that of Kai Grand Guardian, you may add a further 2 to your COMBAT SKILL for the duration of this fight.

If you win the combat, turn to **46**.

### 119

Like a fleeting shadow, you move through the undergrowth towards the brigand leader. As you draw closer, you hear him cursing the incompetence of his men and you see him beating his clenched fist on the trunk of the fallen bough in frustration. Then you leap upon him, covering his mouth with one hand and locking his arm behind his back with the other. He growls and struggles like an angry bear to break free from your grip, but when you whisper a threat in his ear he quickly ceases to resist. Suddenly his nerve seems to break and he begins to whimper like a frightened puppy. You ease your hand away from his mouth just enough so that he can speak and at once he pleads with you not to kill him. He offers you the contents of his satchel and free passage away from here if you will promise not to harm him.

If you wish to see what he has in his satchel, turn to **113**.
If you wish to question him about why he has laid an ambush for you, turn to **75**.

### 120

Swiftly you unshoulder your bow, draw an arrow to your lips, and take hurried aim as the man in black makes his daring leap across the street.

Pick a number from the *Random Number Table*. If you possess the Discipline of Grand Weaponmastery with Bow, add 3 to the number you have picked.

If your total score is now 6 or less, turn to **139**. If it is 7 or more, turn to **328**.

## 121

Soon it is your turn to dip your hand into the trough. As you come to within a few metres of the foul water, you sense that it has been cursed by powerful necromantic spells. The evil surrounding it is strong, and nausea rises up from the pit of your stomach as you dip your fingers into this cursed brine.

Pick a number from the *Random Number Table* (0 = 10). The number you have picked is equal to the number of ENDURANCE points you lose as a result of touching this cursed water.

If your ENDURANCE points total is now 20 or less, turn to **265**.

If your ENDURANCE points total is now 21 or more, turn to **114**.

## 122

You place the food before their feet and step away, but they do not touch it until you sheathe your weapon and taste it yourself to prove that it has not been poisoned (erase this Meal from your *Action Chart*). Ravenously they consume the humble meal in seconds and, when they have finished, they allow you to approach and examine their sickly child. You tell them that you can help their son. Using your innate healing skills, you place your hands upon the boy's chest and let your Kai power flow through into his fever-wracked body. Within a few moments he stirs to consciousness and gives a healthy cry; you have saved his life.

Turn to **277**.

## 123

You whisper the words of the Brotherhood spell 'Lightning Hand' and point your finger at the Arch Druid. A tingling sensation runs down the length of your arm which culminates with a bolt of blue-white energy that arcs from your index finger and explodes against the haft of Cadak's staff.

Your sudden and unexpected use of magic caught the Arch Druid offguard. He defended himself, but you sense that the bolt has weakened him. Seizing this opportunity, you draw your weapon and rush forwards to attack him before he fully recovers.

Arch Druid Cadak:
COMBAT SKILL 48    ENDURANCE 32

If you win this combat, turn to **298**.

## 124

You kneel between two praying acolytes and begin to mumble along with their sonorous prayer-dirge. A shiver runs along your spine and you begin to feel queasy; a strong aura of evil surrounds the group and your psychic senses are struggling to shield your mind from its insidious influence.

You notice that some of the acolytes are shaking uncontrollably, and sweat drips from their faces despite the icy wind which howls across the deck. You recognize that they are suffering the after-effects of using adgana, a potent and highly addictive potion which increases skill and ferocity in combat. You hazard a guess that many of the acolytes were made to take this narcotic before the assault on the quay, to stir them into battle-frenzy.

You have been kneeling among the praying acolytes for barely a minute when suddenly the war-horn blares a long discordant tone. All eyes turn to the east where the shoreline can now be seen on the horizon. The longboat is speeding towards the wooden jetty where a large group of red-robed figures are awaiting its return. The prayer-dirge ceases and everyone gets to their feet in readiness to disembark as soon as the boat docks at the jetty.

Turn to **150**.

## 125

You are awoken in the middle of the night by a tremendous clap of thunder which shakes the ground and startles Bracer. At first you think that a new day must already have dawned, for the cave is awash with bright light. But when you prise open your sleep-clogged eyes and look out over the surrounding landscape, you see that the light has a far sinister origin.

The sky is alive with hordes of glowing, wraith-like phantoms. They swoop down from the roiling storm clouds and skim the treetops, howling and screeching like insane banshees. A trio of these ghastly apparitions pass within a few yards of the cave mouth and suddenly your head is gripped by a crushing pain. You use your Magnakai skills to erect a psi-screen to protect your mind from this psychic attack, but your reflexes are sleep-dulled and you lose 3 ENDURANCE points before your defence is intact.

Turn to **326**.

## 126

Drawing on your mastery of psychic defence, you are able to construct a shield around your mind which absorbs the Elder's probe. He learns nothing from his attempt to read your psyche and, rather than admit to failure, he dismisses you as an empty-headed cretin.

With a growl of disdain, he orders you to rejoin the end of the procession and pushes you out of his way as he strides back to rally those acolytes who are fleeing down the path.

Turn to **250**.

## 127

Using the Brotherhood spell 'Levitation' you are able to rise in the air and glide over this soft section of the cavern floor until you reach firmer ground. With ease, you are then able to slip past the end of the line of automatons and race towards the dais.

During your flight across the sagging floor, the Demoness was putting on an armoured breastplate of varnished black steel and was otherwise distracted. But she saw you get around the flank of her automatons and now she is aware of your plan.

It is clear by the anger on her face that she has no intention of allowing you anywhere near the dais or the Deathstaff.

If you possess Kai-alchemy, turn to **57**.
If you do not possess this Grand Master Discipline, turn to **282**.

### 128

You urge Bracer up a treacherously slick path that leads to the entrance. Without once faltering on the difficult ascent, he carries you to the top of the path where two rusty wagon rails disappear into the mineshaft's shadowy maw. You approach, and the instant you are out of the rain, your keen sixth sense alerts you to the fact that you are not the only ones seeking shelter here. The scent of greasy fur and the glint of two grey-green eyes in the gloom tell you that you have stumbled upon the lair of a mountain wolf.

The wolf growls menacingly and Bracer backs away in fright. Quickly you prepare to use your Magnakai skill of animal control to calm this beast before its hunger or its fear make it attack.

If you possess Animal Mastery, and have reached the rank of Kai Grand Guardian or higher, turn to **89**.
If you do not possess this skill, or have yet to reach this rank, turn instead to **151**.

### 129

Your 'Mind Charm' proves stronger than his will to resist it. With a sigh, he bows his head and becomes completely subservient. Mentally you command him

VII. The scent of greasy fur and the glint of two grey-green
eyes in the gloom . . .

to go and attend to the wounded at the bow of the boat and he obeys at once without question. Those seated around you have now become uncomfortably curious. To avoid their attentions, you get up and move to the stern where a score of acolytes are kneeling in prayer.

Turn to **124**.

## 130

You pass through the arch and feel no harmful effects. But as you descend the steps on the far side, you suddenly notice that a large number of acolytes and Elders are staring at you with hatred and anger in their eyes. You look over your shoulder to see that the invisible curtain of power, through which you passed, is no longer invisible. It is glowing an accusing shade of red.

'Intruder!' screams one of the Elders. 'Unbeliever!' screams another. Then, with a sudden rush, a wave of acolytes comes running at you, many clasping knives and short swords in their fists.

Acolytes of Vasha:
COMBAT SKILL 45    ENDURANCE 40

If you win this combat, turn to **311**.

## 131

Pick a number from the *Random Number Table* (0 = 10). The number you have picked is equal to the number of ENDURANCE points lost as a result of the lightning impact and the fall.

You are left stunned and smouldering by the explosion. Drunkenly, you stagger to your feet and use your Magnakai Discipline of Nexus to extinguish those parts of your cloak and tunic ignited by the blast. Your weapon disintegrated when it was hit (erase it from your *Action Chart*), yet it served to conduct some of the energy of the lightning ball away from your body.

Your terrified horse has halted at the river's edge and you call to him, using your natural Kai skills to calm and control his fear. He responds at once and returns to collect you. Swiftly you climb back into the saddle and gallop away along the river trail, anxious to put distance between you and this deadly storm.

Turn to **80**.

### 132

At Shamath's command, her attendants draw wicked-looking slivers of steel from scabbards hidden inside their robes and, with a cry of vengeance, they come rushing forwards to hack you down.

Cheghath: COMBAT SKILL 37    ENDURANCE 40

These beings are gifted with strong psychic defences. Halve all bonuses you would normally receive if you choose to use a psychic attack (including Kai Blast) during this combat.

If you win the combat, turn to **303**.

### 133

You accept the package and carefully unfold its silken wrapper to reveal an amulet, oblong in shape, strung upon a length of crude twine. It has been carved from coal-black stone, flecked with grains of metal, which sparkle in the firelight.

'Where was this found?' you ask.

'In the ruins of Vorn,' replies Kadharian, ominously.

> If you possess the Discipline of Telegnosis, and have reached the Kai rank of Sun Knight or higher, turn to **262**.
> If you do not possess this Discipline, or have yet to reach this level of Kai mastery, turn to **49**.

## 134

Your punch knocks the Elder off his feet and leaves him slumped unconscious against the gunwale. A deathly silence descends on the deck and all eyes turn to stare in disbelief at what you have done.

'Seize him!' bellows another Elder, and a score of acolytes spring from the benches to obey the command. You draw your weapon and fight them with breathtaking skill and valour, but eventually you are overcome by the sheer weight of numbers. By the time they have disarmed you and pinned you to the deck, more than thirty of them lie slain or seriously injured in a heaped circle around where you lie.

You stare back defiantly at the ring of grim faces that loom over you. Then the face of an acolyte Elder comes into view and he sneers with disdain when he sees that you are a Sommlending. He places the tip of his glowing wand to your forehead and suddenly there is an explosion of white light. Sadly, it is the last sensation you will ever experience.

Your life and your quest end here.

## 135

You draw the Sommerswerd from its scabbard and point it accusingly at the Arch Druid, expecting him to wither in the face of its goodly light. But the blade does not glow as radiantly as before: it is as if its powers are being subdued by Cadak's spectral prison.

With loathing in your heart, you advance upon your despised enemy. He weaves his hands before his face and his image fades. He is using a spell of invisibility but it does not keep him entirely hidden: you can still see the outline of his staff and his body flickering as he moves against the background wall of light.

Arch Druid Cadak:
COMBAT SKILL 50    ENDURANCE 35

If you win this combat, turn to **298**.

## 136

You retreat into the copse, using your Magnakai skills of invisibility to keep you hidden from the advancing brigands. In their clumsy eagerness to enter the trees, they fail to notice you slip through their lines and circle around behind them. You have outwitted them but you are still anxious that they may find your horse. You move to higher ground in order to get a better view of the copse and, from a vantage point among the boulders, you observe their leader and three of his henchmen hiding nearby, crouched behind the bough of a fallen tree.

If you possess a Bow and wish to fire an arrow at the brigand leader, turn to **304**.

If you possess Kai-alchemy and wish to use the spell of 'Mind Charm', turn to **212**.

If you decide to wait and observe the brigands a little longer, turn to **98**.

### 137

As you approach the hall, you notice that it has only one means of entry — a large pair of double doors facing the lake. A long procession of acolytes are filing into the hall through these open doors and you stop to observe them. It occurs to you that if you are to discover what is going on inside, then you will have to enter by the same way.

A portly perimeter guard passes by and you duck into a darkened doorway to avoid being seen. He goes into a hut opposite and suddenly an idea springs to mind, an idea that could get you into the grand hall. You hurry across to the hut and rush in, catching the acolyte by surprise. A blow to the back of the head renders him unconscious and quickly you put on his voluminous red robes which completely cover your clothing and equipment (you need not record these robes on your *Action Chart*).

Dressed as an acolyte, and aided by your Kai camouflage skills, you should now have no difficulty getting into the hall.

If, before leaving the hut, you wish to search it for useful items, turn to **289**.

If you do not, turn to **143**.

## 138

You wield the Deathstaff with strength and confidence. The whirling cyclone ruins the vortexi attack and bleeds them of their psychic powers, rendering them harmless.

However, by using the Deathstaff to accomplish this, you have left yourself vulnerable to its insidious power: lose 3 ENDURANCE points.

Make the necessary adjustments to your *Action Chart* and turn to **46**.

## 139

You let fly your arrow but it is poorly aimed. It arcs harmlessly into the night sky as the archer lands on the roof of the building opposite. Determined not to let him get away, you dash along the street, your eyes fixed on the shadowy figure as he makes his escape across the rooftops of the north quarter. You are twenty metres ahead of him when the street makes a turn and you find yourself faced by a solid brick wall; you have come to a dead end. You are about to retrace your steps when suddenly you notice a rusty iron staircase away to your right. It is a crude fire-escape ladder and it leads all the way to the roof of a linen warehouse. Quickly you climb the ladder, your weapon drawn in readiness to intercept the assassin the moment he appears.

Turn to **95**.

### 140

You unsheathe your weapon and brace yourself to receive their maniacal attack.

Acolytes of Vashna (in battle frenzy):
COMBAT SKILL 34    ENDURANCE 40

If you win this combat, turn to **325**.

### 141

Suddenly, a sparkling sheet of energy shimmers beneath the great arch, and you catch sight of a huge, booted foot stepping through it. You tremble at the thought of what will happen next, for you recognize only too well to whom the foot belongs. With mounting horror you watch as the Demoness Shamath emerges from the shadow gate in her entirety. Here on Magnamund she is five times greater in size and power than in her own domain, and she is hungry to exercise that terrible power.

She stoops down and plucks the Deathstaff from you as if she was removing a tiny splinter of wood from a lowly insect. Then she points a tree-sized finger at the ground before the dais and a huge hole appears.

A raging whirlwind arises from this abyss, a whirling vortex which quickly builds in power until it is sucking everything into its spinning black core. Screaming acolytes tumble past and disappear into its maw as you desperately hang on to the dais to stop yourself from being sucked to your death. But your resistance is futile. With a callous flick of her wrist, the Demoness Shamath consigns you to your doom.

Tragically, your life and your quest end here.

### 142

You draw your weapon and brace yourself as the phantoms swoop down upon you like hungry vultures descending on a corpse.

> Vortexi: COMBAT SKILL 46    ENDURANCE 40

For every level of Kai rank you have attained above that of Kai Grand Guardian, you may add 2 to your COMBAT SKILL for the duration of this fight. If you possess the Sommerswerd, add 5 to your ENDURANCE points score.

If you win the combat, turn to **159**.

### 143

You raise the hood of your robe and join the procession of acolytes who are filing into the hall. The interior is a dark and forbidding place, decorated with the ritualistic trappings of the acolytes of Vashna. Spluttering candles dimly illuminate a central altar and a sickly-smelling incense saturates the air. The acolytes encircle the altar several ranks deep and listen intently as two of their Elders conduct a liturgy in praise of Darklord Vashna, and the victory he has seen fit to grant them. They conclude their sinister ceremony by crying out the words, 'we celebrate this eve of the "Great Welcoming". May Lord Vashna, our master, vanquish his enemies and rule unchallenged ever more!'

The acolytes respond spontaneously by repeatedly chanting their master's name. 'Vashna! Vashna! Vashna!' they cry, as they slowly shuffle out of the hall in single file. At the door, each acolyte is handed a burning torch and made to parade past the Elders who give them their unholy blessing. You take care to keep your face concealed within the raised hood of your robe as your turn comes to pass before them.

Pick a number from the *Random Number Table*. If you possess Kai-alchemy, Kai-screen, or Assimilance, add 2 to the number you have picked.

Also, if you possess a Runic Disc, add 1; if you possess the Sommerswerd, deduct 3; and for every rank you have attained above that of Kai Grand Guardian, add 1.

If your total score is now 4 or less, turn to **322**.
If it is 5 or more, turn to **192**.

## 144

As the screaming vortexi horde swoop down, you pray to Kai and Ishir to give you strength enough to defeat them.

If you possess the Sommerswerd, turn to **118**.
If you do not possess this Special Item, turn to **284**.

## 145

As the first of the brigand captain's men emerge from the surrounding pines, you break off the fight and take to your heels, pausing only to snatch up his satchel as you leave. Thinking that his swordsmanship has terrified you into running away, the captain gives chase, but he soon loses you among the dense pines and gives up his pursuit.

Turn to **247**.

## 146

Suddenly, a grey-haired man dressed in furs springs up from behind the boulder with a loaded crossbow clutched in his hands.

'Don't move!' he growls, and levels the weapon at your heart.

If you possess the Discipline of Telegnosis, and wish to use it, turn to **201**.

If you do not possess this skill, or choose not to use it, turn to **280**.

## 147

The street ends at a stagnant fountain where a rowdy crowd has gathered to watch a bare-knuckled contest between two tough streetfighters. You stop to ask one of the spectators the way to the Crooked Sage Inn and, somewhat to your surprise, he seems pleased to offer his help. He gives you clear directions to Tavern Lane, the street where the inn is situated, and less than ten minutes later you find yourself at a signpost which marks the start of this narrow thoroughfare.

Turn to **332**.

## 148

Shamath recoils in horror before your deadly blows. She begins to whimper. Then, quite suddenly, a geyser of flame shoots from the ground and engulfs her worm-like body. You watch with disbelief as the tendrilled flesh blackens and flakes away in a matter of seconds, to leave nothing but a coiled heap of glowing cinders on the mirrored floor.

Turn to **261**.

## 149

The bolt streaks towards you and, for one terrible moment, you are frozen rigid with fear. Then your natural Kai instincts take command and suddenly it is as if everything is happening in slow motion. You are in mortal danger and must act swiftly if you are to survive.

If you possess Kai-alchemy and wish to use it, turn to **71**.

If you do not, you can attempt to avoid the bolt by diving out of the building. Turn to **7**.

## 150

The longboat glides to a halt beside the jetty and attendant acolytes make it secure with ropes and hawsers. An Elder oversees the disembarkation, allowing the wounded off first, followed by the rest in descending order of rank and superiority. You join in the queue with the lowly initiates and follow the line as it files off the jetty and up a torchlit hilltrack to a hall of stone. It is a grand building which shows signs of having only recently been constructed.

The interior of the hall is a dark and forbidding place, decorated with the ritualistic trappings of the acolytes of Vashna. Spluttering candles dimly illuminate a central altar and a sickly-smelling incense saturates the air. The acolytes encircle the altar several ranks deep and listen intently as two of their Elders conduct a liturgy in praise of Darklord Vashna, and the victory he has seen fit to grant them. They conclude their sinister ceremony by crying out the words, 'We celebrate this eve of the "Great Welcoming". May Lord Vashna, our master, vanquish his enemies and rule unchallenged ever more!'

The acolytes respond spontaneously by repeatedly chanting their master's name. 'Vashna! Vashna! Vashna!' they cry, as they slowly shuffle out of the hall in single file. At the door, each acolyte is handed a burning torch and made to parade past the Elders who give them their unholy blessing. You take care to keep your face concealed within the raised hood of your robe as your turn comes to pass before them.

Pick a number from the *Random Number Table*. If you possess Kai-alchemy, Kai-screen, or Assimilance, add 2 to the number you have picked.

Also, if you possess a Runic Disc, add 1; if you possess the Sommerswerd, deduct 3; and for every rank you have attained above that of Kai Grand Guardian, add 1.

If your total score is now 4 or less, turn to **322**. If it is 5 or more, turn to **192**.

### 151

Your basic Kai skills are sufficient to calm the wolf, but he is clearly agitated by the scent and presence of your horse. Confused and frustrated by its conflicting instincts, the wolf retreats into the depths of the mineshaft where it howls throughout the remainder of the night.

Unable to sleep because of the wolf's incessant cries, you spend the next five hours in quiet discomfort waiting for the storm to subside: lose 2 ENDURANCE points.

Turn to **279**.

### 152

You unsheathe your weapon and wait with bated breath as you listen to the beast approaching. It sounds as if it is more than thirty metres away when suddenly, with a deafening roar, it drops through the fog and lands upon you. Desperately you fight to defend yourself as it tries to rake you unmercifully with fang and claw.

VIII.  You unsheathe your weapon and wait with baited
breath as you listen to the beast approaching.

Zarthyn: COMBAT SKILL 45    ENDURANCE 50

If you win this combat, turn to **90**.

**153**

You back away from the advancing line of automatons and try to use your speed and agility to get around their flank. But you have taken less than a dozen steps when you feel the floor becoming soft and spongy beneath your feet.

If you possess Telegnosis, and have reached the Kai rank of Sun Lord, turn to **193**.

If you possess Kai-alchemy, and wish to use it, turn to **127**.

If you do not possess these skills, or if you have yet to attain the rank of Sun Lord, turn to **232**.

## 154

You fly through the air towards the opposite roof, yet in your haste to pursue the assassin, you misjudge the jump and land short. Desperately, you scrabble to get a grip on the rusty guttering at the edge of the tiled roof, but it is weak and cannot support your weight. It collapses and, with a cry of fear, you plummet backwards into the street below.

Turn to **38**.

## 155

The trail meanders away from the lapping waters of the lake and winds slowly upwards to a chalky plateau covered with dense scrub. Clumps of dull yellow blossoms, blighted by the severe weather, cling to the boughs of this foliage. They give off a pleasant odour which your horse finds irresistible. You sense that they are nutritious and so you stop and both of you eat your fill: restore 3 ENDURANCE points. (There is a sufficient surplus of blossoms for 2 Meals.)

Turn to **338**.

## 156

Throughout the afternoon, the rocky trail descends through an unlovely landscape of shale hills and crags topped with thorny brambles. It is difficult terrain but your ride passes without incident. Shortly before dusk, you come to the top of a ridge and catch your first glimpse of the River Storn and the snow-capped peaks of the southern Durncrags beyond. The elation of having come this far is sobered when you see that the distant sky is changing rapidly, and only a slender streak of light fringes the horizon. A storm is closing in.

As you make the long, gradual descent towards the river, the air becomes humid and dark clouds appear overhead. The turmoil of moisture quickly charges the atmosphere. Lightning flashes without warning from the clouds to the earth and arcs skyward again, its energy echoing in a slow roll of thunder. Then the heavens open and a deluge of rain saturates the land. You calm your startled horse and urge him through the pouring rain, praying all the while that you will be able to find shelter before night closes in.

You are within a mile of the river when the darkness is almost complete. Yet, aided by your keen vision, you are able to make out two places that can offer some degree of shelter from the storm. The first is a cone-shaped stone hut, perched near the river's edge; the second is a rocky hollow close to the trail.

If you wish to shelter in the hut, turn to **207**.

If you wish to take shelter in the rocky hollow, turn to **91**.

## 157

You scramble to your feet and sprint to the dais where you wrench the Deathstaff from the floor of the lower tier. To your horror it feels abnormally heavy and you sag beneath its weight. The

Demoness spins around and emits a terrible scream when she sees what you are holding. The noise of her wrath lifts you bodily and sends you skidding across the floor.

Desperately, you fight to maintain your grip on the Deathstaff as the furious Shamath comes striding towards you. The deafening shriek of her voice rings once more in your ears as you clutch the Deathstaff to your chest and take a running leap into the dark oblivion of the shadow gate.

Turn to **270**.

## 158

You scan the brooding sky, using your ability to see in the ultraviolet and infrared light spectrums. Your advanced Kai skills enable you to see and track the flying creatures as they circle slowly around their lair and come swooping down to attack you.

You draw your weapon and, in the ultraviolet spectrum, you detect that an aura of protection is sheathing it from the extreme temperature of this domain. Then a hideous shriek splits the air as the first of the beasts dives upon you.

Lavas: COMBAT SKILL 44    ENDURANCE 42

You may evade this combat after five rounds, by turning to **276**.

If you win the combat, turn to **3**.

## 159

You have destroyed all of the ghostly creatures that were attacking you, but you are mindful that there are still hundreds of these malevolent spirits circling the area. You stand with your horse at the rear of the shallow cave, your weapon ready in hand, and pray to Kai and Ishir to keep you both safely hidden. Gleefully, the vortexi ride the raging storm for more than an hour until eventually it dies and they slowly disappear.

An uneasy calm descends upon the land. You sense that the danger has passed and try to get some rest, but the recent memory of your ghastly confrontation is still vivid in your mind and it makes it impossible for you to sleep: lose 3 ENDURANCE points.

Furthermore, unless you possess Grand Hunt-mastery, you must now eat a Meal or lose an additional 3 ENDURANCE points.

Turn to **337**.

**160**

The Elder's probe breaks through your defence and he suddenly realizes that you are an intruder. He pulls at your robe and tears it open, revealing your leather tunic and breeches. Recognizing them at once to be Sommlending in origin, he gasps with shock as he guesses at your true identity.

'Seize him!' he bellows, and a score of acolytes spring forward to obey the command. You draw your weapon and fight them with breathtaking skill and valour, but eventually you are overcome by the sheer weight of their numbers. By the time they have disarmed you and pinned you to the rocky ground, more than thirty of them lie slain or seriously injured in a heaped circle around where you lie.

You stare back defiantly at the ring of grim torchlit faces that loom over you. Then the face of the Elder comes into view and he sneers with disdain. He places the tip of a glowing wand to your forehead and suddenly there is an explosion of white light. Sadly for you, it is the last sensation you will ever experience.

Your life and your quest end here, on the trail to the Maakengorge.

## 161

The shops and hovels which sandwich this narrow street show no visible signs of life. Heavy iron bars and stout oaken shutters secure their every portal, understandably a necessary precaution in this villainous city. You are beginning to lose hope of finding the Crooked Sage Inn, when suddenly you notice a pale yellow light streaming from the doorway of a nearby building. As you ride closer, you see a sign hanging above the door. It shows a black bear standing upright on its hind legs, and in its forepaws it grasps a placard which says:

GHADLAR & SONS — FURRIERS

If you wish to enter the furrier's shop, turn to **226**.
If you choose to ignore it, you may continue along this street by turning to **244**.

## 162

The howling phantoms come swirling out of the storm. They encircle the great shimmering arch in a long, unbroken chain, and then, one by one, they peel away to dive at the place where you are standing. Guided by your Kai instincts, you raise the Deathstaff and whirl it around your head — once, twice, three times . . .

An ominous hum radiates from its haft. There is a crackle of static electricity and the damp air seethes with restrained, undischarged power. A thread of mist issues from the staff's tip and builds rapidly into a spinning cyclone that ensnares the vortexi and prevents them from reaching you. In desperation, you sense them pooling their immense psychic energies in an attempt to break out of this whirling prison and attack you.

Pick a number from the *Random Number Table*.

If you possess Kai-surge, add 4 to this number. If you possess Kai-screen, add 2. If you possess Assimilance, add 1.

Also, if your current ENDURANCE points total is 18 or more, add 1; if your current ENDURANCE points total is 17 or less, deduct 1.

If your total score is now *3* or less, turn to **206**.
If it is *4–8*, turn to **305**.
If it is *9* or more, turn to **138**.

### 163

Tied to a stone obelisk in the centre of the quay square are three acolytes of Vashna. They are guarded by two Vakovarian brigands who keep themselves amused by bullying and tormenting them.

For the past hour the sky overhead has become increasingly grey and thundery, with occasional storm flashes illuminating the northern shore. Now this storm is crossing the lake and the lightning is beginning to strike dangerously close to the quay. The brigands seemingly ignore this danger, so preoccupied are they with their petty cruelties, but then something appears on the surface of the lake which commands their attention.

A massive bank of grey-white fog is rolling across the water towards the quay at an unnatural pace. When it is just a few hundred metres from the shore, a volley of lightning bolts comes hurtling from its core to explode against the quayside wall with devastating effect. Several brigands are incinerated where they stand, leaving nothing but glowing piles of ash to mark their passing. Then, suddenly, a massive longboat emerges from the wall of fog and comes speeding towards the quay. Glowing bolts of energy dart from its prow to explode upon the deck of the Vakovarian ship. One of these bolts passes high between the masts and arcs through the air towards

IX. Suddenly, a massive longboat emerges from the wall of fog and comes speeding towards the quay.

the quay. You watch with mounting horror as it comes speeding directly towards you.

If you possess the Sommerswerd, turn to **176**.
If you do not possess this Special Item, turn to **149**.

### 164

Galvanized into action by the fear of what will happen should the Demoness be allowed entry to this world, you cast your eyes and Kai senses across the symbols which are engraved upon the crystal surface of the uppermost tier. Then, in a sudden flash of inspiration, you realize that the symbols themselves are the key to the activation of the shadow gate.

You study the symbols and determine that a sequence must be completed in order for you to be able to close the shadow gate.

Study the following grid of numbers carefully. When you think you know the missing number, turn to the entry which bears the same number as your answer.

| 6 | 4 | 3 | X | 5 |
|---|---|---|---|---|
| 2 | 5 |   | 4 | 9 |
| 4 | 3 | 4 | X | X |

If you cannot solve the problem, turn to **235**.

## 165

You throw yourself flat against Bracer's neck and the bolt parts your hair as it whistles past your head. Unharmed, you reach the cover of a dense pine copse where you quickly dismount. Having secured Bracer's reins to a tree, you move back to the edge of the copse to try and catch a glimpse of your attackers. You have no difficulty seeing them: a dozen brigands, armed with crossbows and swords, are rushing through the undergrowth directly towards your hiding place.

If you possess a Bow and wish to use it, turn to **330**.

If you do not, turn to **136**.

## 166

The moment you step through the archway you feel an electrifying jolt run through your body, and snake-like tendrils of blue-white energy arc from the rim of the arch to the hilt of the Sommerswerd. A gasp of astonishment arises from the acolytes, audible even above the howling wind.

'We have an intruder in our midst,' screams Cadak, levelling his wizard's staff at you accusingly. You fight the paralysing effect of the current and tug the sun-sword free of its scabbard. For a moment the current weakens as it is absorbed and neutralized by the Sommerswerd's divine energy, but then the tip of Cadak's staff ignites with a crimson flame and the current intensifies anew, numbing your limbs with its insidious effect.

'Ha! I know you, intruder,' yells Cadak, maniacally, 'You are Lone Wolf, the doomed hero of a doomed realm. You are a fool to come here, Kai lord. Your powers are no match for those of Naar, the King of the Darkness.'

With this he turns to the acolytes and throws up his hands triumphantly.

'This night we shall celebrate a double victory, my brethren. The resurrection of Lord Vashna and the destruction of Grand Master Lone Wolf!'

The acolytes scream their approval, but their cheer is drowned by the ever-increasing noise of the storm. Then you see that the storm itself is changing. A huge vortex of whirling cloud is descending from the heavens, a tornado whose deadly funnel is reaching down towards you. Then the tip of the roaring plume touches the ground at your feet and, with a terrifying suddenness, you are torn from the energy curtain and sent hurtling through the air towards the dark centre of the towering arch.

Turn to **60**.

## 167

You cease firing, having decided to conserve your remaining arrows for later. After a few minutes the brigands suspect that one of their bolts has found its mark and they come creeping forwards.

You retreat into the copse, using your Magnakai skills of invisibility to keep you hidden from the advancing brigands. They pass you, enabling you to circle around behind them. You have outwitted them but you are still anxious that they may find Bracer. You move to higher ground in order to get a better view of the copse and, from a vantage point among the boulders, you observe their leader and three of his henchmen hiding nearby, crouched behind the bough of a fallen tree.

> If you wish to fire an arrow at the brigand leader, turn to **304**.
>
> If you possess Kai-alchemy and wish to use the spell of 'Mind Charm', turn to **212**.
>
> If you decide to wait and observe the brigands a little longer, turn to **98**.

### 168

You hurry down towards the circle of boulders, dragging your frozen horse behind you, eager to get him out of this icy gale. You are twenty metres from your goal when you are brought skidding to a halt by your hunting senses — something is wrong here. You listen and, to your horror, you detect the clacking of fangs and the scent of blood and greasy fur. Suddenly the clacking ceases and a terrifying howl arises from the far side of the boulders.

> If you wish to mount your horse and gallop away from here, turn to **309**.
>
> If you choose to draw your weapon and investigate what lurks on the other side of these boulders, turn to **208**.

### 169

'Easy, Smudd,' you say, letting your hands drift away from your weapons, 'I mean you no harm. I just want to talk with you awhile, that's all.'

The scrawny-faced knave looks at you with deep

suspicion, his hand tightening around the hilt of his rapier.

'Look,' you say, reaching for your money pouch, 'I'm even prepared to pay for the privilege.'

Slowly you remove five Gold Crowns and place them on the table (if you currently have less than five Gold Crowns, you give Smudd what you have *plus* one item from your Backpack).

Adjust your *Action Chart* accordingly, then turn to **323**.

## 170

You barely manage to utter the words of the spell before the deadly bolt slams into the magical shield. For a moment you are blinded by a splash of sparks which blister your face (lose 2 ENDURANCE points), but you quickly recover and urge your horse onwards with renewed vigour.

Turn to **5**.

## 171

Inspired by your plan, you run towards the advancing line of automatons, taking care to keep a watchful eye on Demoness Shamath, and your goal – the distant Deathstaff.

Pick a number from the *Random Number Table*.

If you possess Assimilance, add 2 to the number you have picked. If you possess Grand Pathsmanship, add 1. If you possess Telegnosis, add 1. Also, for every level of Kai mastery you have attained above the rank of Kai Grand Defender, add 1.

If your total score is now 5 or less, turn to **334**.
If it is 6 or more, turn to **34**.

## 172

The crossing is laborious and tiring (lose 2 ENDURANCE points), but at length you reach the far side of the river and disembark safely. A stony trail runs along the bank, heading north, and you follow it with high hopes of reaching Lake Vorndarol before sunset.

All day the sun blazes supreme in a cloudless sky and waves of heat create a shimmering, distorted view of the trail ahead. The distant horizon is streaked with myriad colours and the dry air crackles with electricity, a legacy of last night's violent storm. Late in the afternoon you come to the ruins of an ancient settlement and stop here to allow your horse to rest awhile in the shade.

If you possess Grand Pathsmanship, turn to **102**.
If you do not possess this Discipline, turn to **260**.

## 173

The young woman smiles at you and begins to laugh.

'You can't harm me, Lone Wolf,' she says, full of confidence. 'You may as well sheathe that weapon for now, though you'll be needing it later I fancy.'

'Who are you? What do you want?' you hiss, still clutching your weapon defensively. 'Are you some cursed illusion, some mind-trick of Naar's sent to entrap me? Well, demon, maybe this will wipe the smile off your face.'

You strike the young woman a savage blow to the head but to no effect. She laughs again and says, with a mocking tone, 'Now do you believe me?'

You back away, looking to either side for a way of escaping this creature, but there is none. She advances, and you regard her with fearful caution. She is wearing a worn leather jerkin and ragged trousers which are cut short at the knees, and does not appear to be armed with a weapon.

'You should be more respectful,' she says, 'after all, if I should decide to leave, who'll keep you hidden from the gaze of Shamath?' She points to the giant demoness to illustrate who she means. 'Trinket or no,' she continues, motioning to the Platinum Amulet you wear, 'you wouldn't last long against her without my help.'

'What do you want from me?' you reply, uneasily.

'Your attention would be a good start. Strange as it may seem, I wish to help you, Lone Wolf.'

If you possess Telegnosis, turn to **221**.
If you do not possess this Discipline, turn to **286**.

### 174

On leaving the furrier's shop, you continue along the street until you reach a junction. The old woman's directions lead you through a warren of covered alleyways and narrow passages which eventually lead to the start of Tavern Lane, the street where she says you'll find the Crooked Sage Inn.

Turn to **332**.

**175**

You collect your horse and accompany Fyrad to his camp which is hidden in a hill cave. The hunter has made this bare rock hollow surprisingly comfortable with a fire, a straw mattress, and a rock-lined food store dug into its earthen floor. The two corvayl pelts he spoke of are hanging on wooden frames near the smouldering embers of the fire, and his mule, which he calls 'Izzy', is dozing at the rear of the cave.

As you enter, a hawk swoops down from the roof and lands on Fyrad's arm. He produces a strip of dried meat from his pocket and the hawk takes it back to his perch to consume at his leisure.

'Fine bird, that 'un,' he says, fondly. 'He's led me to some rich quarry over the years.'

Over a meal of rabbit and wild berries, you ask Fyrad what he knows about the acolytes of Vashna and the Maakengorge. He says he has seen their camp on the east shore of the lake but, like the infamous gorge, only from a distance. His main cause for concern has been the storms and the Vakovarian bandits. If he did not have a hungry family and debts to meet in Karkaste, he would have packed up and gone home a month ago.

After your delicious meal, you attend to your horse before settling down for the night. You offer to share the watch but Fyrad says this will not be necessary.

'Best watchman you could ever wish for,' he says, pointing to his pet hawk. 'He'll let us know in good time if trouble comes a-callin' tonight.'

Turn to **66**.

X.  As you enter, a hawk swoops down from the roof and
      lands on Fyrad's arm.

## 176

You unsheathe the sun-sword and strike out at the approaching bolt in a desperate attempt to deflect it away. It strikes the edge of the blade and you are blinded by an eruption of searing white light. The Sommerswerd has negated the force of the bolt, rendering it harmless, but the shock of the impact sends you reeling backwards. As you fall you knock your head on a charred timber: lose 2 ENDURANCE points.

To continue, turn to **200**.

## 177

A grimace spreads slowly across the Elder's face and sweat breaks out on his forehead as he tries to shut you out of his mind. Suddenly, he breaks the spell and his mouth opens wide. In your desperation to prevent him from sounding the alarm, you lash out with your clenched fist and punch him squarely on the jaw.

Pick a number from the *Random Number Table*.

If the number you have picked is *0–4*, turn to **333**.
If it is *5–9*, turn to **134**.

## 178

Gwynian leads you into the derelict hovel and offers you a seat next to an ancient table carved from stone. Then he lowers himself carefully into a chair opposite and looks deeply into your eyes.

'Lord Rimoah sent word to me in Varetta that you were on your way here,' he says, taking a parchment envelope from the folds of his robes. 'I, and my fellow sages, have been observing the skies in this region for many months, and we are sure that an event of great and terrible importance is close at hand. The stars and the storms portend that an evil power is soon to appear on Magnamund.'

'Could it be the rising of Vashna?' you ask, daring to voice your fear.

'Yes, we believe it to be Vashna. Unless you can prevent it, Lone Wolf, the Darklord and his army will rise from the Maakengorge.'

If you possess a Black Amulet, turn to **234**.
If you do not possess this Special Item, turn to **45**.

## 179

Shamath's laughter becomes a hideous screech. She mouths a word of power and a flood of psychic energy comes washing across the cavern towards you. Fortunately, it hits the force field and breaks like a wave against it, sparing you from its full effect. Even so, the residue which penetrates the wall is enough to leave you stunned and gasping for breath: lose 3 ENDURANCE points.

The Demoness flicks her fingers and instantly the wall is gone. But now you see that you are surrounded by a ring of her sinister, robed attendants.

If you possess the Sommerswerd, turn to **58**.
If you do not possess this Special Item, turn to **97**.

## 180

The birds attack at such a tremendous speed that you dismiss the idea of using a bow. Swiftly you draw your weapon — it has barely cleared its sheath when the first of the scavengers swoop in for the kill. You are forced to release your grip on the guide rope and step back a few paces for you are not the target of their attack; they are after your horse.

Durncrag scavengers:
COMBAT SKILL 42     ENDURANCE 18

If you win this combat, turn to **317**.


### 181

Your psychic defence holds fast and the Elder learns nothing from his attempt to read your mind. Rather than admit to failure, he curses and denounces you as an empty-headed cretin.

With a growl of disdain, he orders you to rejoin the procession and pushes you roughly out of his way as he strides back to his position beside the altar.

Turn to **250**.


### 182

Swiftly you steer Bracer off the track and into the surrounding undergrowth. Almost immediately you hear an angry voice shouting a command, followed by the sound of crossbow bolts in flight. A glance over your shoulder makes your heart leap — a bolt is speeding directly towards your face!

If you possess Kai-alchemy, turn to **170**.
If you do not possess this Grand Master Discipline, turn to **69**.

## 183

You draw an arrow to your lips and fire it with blinding speed and accuracy. It pierces the heart of the leading acolyte, killing him instantly, and causes his partner to skid to a halt. Unnerved by your deadly prowess with a bow, he turns and runs towards his brethren who are fighting at the quayside.

Erase one arrow from your *Action Chart*, and turn to **325**.

## 184

You turn your head slightly and see a pair of sandalled feet standing on the deck by your side. They belong to the Elder whom you almost collided with when you jumped aboard the longboat. He repeats his command and this time you recognize some of the words. You think he is saying something like: 'Move, or you'll be wounded.'

If you wish to move along the bench, turn to **219**.
If you decide to ignore his command, turn to **292**.

## 185

'Bah! Y' towheaded screwjaws,' curses the drunkard, when you refuse to pay his outrageous price. 'I've more pressin' things t' do than waste breath on you.'

With this, he stumbles away into the fog, clutching his jug of ale. You watch him disappear, then you look again at the three exits from this square and try to fathom which one will lead you to the Crooked Sage Inn.

If you wish to leave the square by the north exit, turn to **16**.

If you wish to leave the square by the east exit, turn to **332**.

If you wish to leave the square by the west exit, turn to **161**.

## 186

It seems that the closer you get to the pool, the hotter the relic becomes. Another few steps and it will be hot enough to explode. Desperately, you fumble to retrieve it from the charred pocket of your tunic, and hurl it away.

Pick a number from the *Random Number Table*.

If the number you have picked is *0–4*, turn to **96**. If it is *5–9*, turn to **316**.

## 187

In the distance you see a dim light flickering and twinkling at the heart of these ice mountains. You strike out towards it, across the frost-encrusted ground, and find yourself covering the distance far quicker than would ever be possible on Magnamund. A kilometre slips by at a single step and the surrounding terrain becomes impossible to focus on. Suspecting that you are the victim of some powerful illusion, you stride up to the flickering ice wall and thrust your hand against it. Effortlessly, your palm sinks into the glassy blue surface and you fall headlong into the icy mountainside.

Turn to **44**.

## 188

As the last of the Vakovarians falls dead at your feet, you step away from their heaped bodies and wipe the sweat of battle from your bloodied brow. You have slain the enemy but you can hear more of their kind crashing through the undergrowth, eager to reach you and avenge the deaths of their brothers-in-arms.

Several of the dead have satchels, quivers and backpacks slung about their shoulders. Some have been torn open during the combat and their contents lie spilled out on the ground. A cursory glance reveals the following weapons and other items:

6 Arrows
Comb
Broadsword
Dagger
Pipe
Sword
Spyglass
Enough food for 3 Meals
Blanket
20 Gold Crowns

If you wish to keep any of these items, remember to mark them on your *Action Chart*.

Swiftly you make your escape into the dense pines. The area is alive with bandits and you are forced to flee northwards, away from the place where you left Bracer tethered to a tree. You are anxious for his safety and mindful that there are still many miles to be covered before you reach Lake Vorndarol, but you dare not turn back for him. Then you hear something that makes you halt in your tracks: it is the sound of a horse whinnying.

Turn to **223**.

## 189

'Attend with care to what I say, mortal,' says the face of Shamath. 'When I have finished, I shall ask you this question: "While I am here to do Naar's bidding, how many loyal servants guard my throne of power?"'

Shamath notes the look of concentration on your face and she allows herself a sneering laugh at your expense before she continues. She is confident that you will not defeat her in this intellectual contest. She begins:

'In addition to the loyal servants, there are two Dwellers of the Abyss.

'When the loyal servants and the Dwellers of the Abyss were counted together, their total number was doubled when my Lieutenants of Night arrived.

'But when my Lieutenants of Night arrived, the Dwellers of the Abyss had to leave.

'Exactly half of the remaining number also departed, for they were beholden to the Dwellers.'

'From the remainder I picked the loyal servants to guard my throne of power. I chose them all, except for one who was known to me as a traitor. I executed the traitor before I set my loyal servants to guard my throne.

'So, mortal, answer my question: while I am here to do Naar's bidding, how many loyal servants guard my throne of power?'

Study the words of Shamath's riddle carefully. When you think you have the answer, turn to the entry which bears the same number as your answer.

If you cannot answer Shamath's riddle, turn to **216**.

**190**

Suddenly the Elder grabs your robe and pulls it open, revealing your leather tunic, cloak and breeches. Recognizing them at once to be Sommlending in origin, he gasps with shock as he guesses your true identity.

Turn to **314**.

### 191

You watch from the edge of the warehouse roof as the assassin makes his escape. For a moment he halts beside a tall chimney stack and turns to look in your direction. Then three other shadowy figures emerge from behind the stack and stand at his shoulder. They stare at you silently for a few moments before turning and melting away into the night.

Having decided not to follow, you make your way down from the warehouse roof and retrace your steps back to the stables of the Crooked Sage to collect your horse.

Turn to **341**.

### 192

You pass before the Elders without incident and follow the procession as it winds its way through the settlement. As it nears the perimeter, you pass beside some smaller huts where a few of the doors are open. Most of the huts are empty, but you notice one where a table near the door is stacked with captured weapons.

If you wish to slip away from the procession and enter this weapons hut, turn to **24**.

If you do not, turn to **218**.

### 193

Using your advanced Kai mastery, you alter your body weight so that you are able to glide over this soft section of the cavern floor and you soon reach firmer ground. With ease, you slip past the end of the line of automatons and race towards the dais.

During your flight across the sagging floor, the Demoness was putting on an armoured breastplate of varnished black steel and was otherwise distracted. But she saw you get around the flank of her automatons and now she is aware of your plan. It is clear by the anger on her face that she has no intention of allowing you anywhere near the dais or the Deathstaff.

If you possess Kai-alchemy, turn to **57**.
If you do not possess this Grand Master Discipline, turn to **282**.

### 194

Your spine tingles with the presentiment of danger. Your senses warn that something evil is abroad this night and you are fearful that it will come upon you while you are sleeping. With this worry foremost in your mind, you stand at the mouth of the cave and use your Kai mastery to summon a woodland creature. A few minutes pass, then you sight a wildcat and its cub emerging from the pines. They have answered your call and obediently they submit to your will. You command them to guard the cave mouth, then you settle down to rest, confident in the knowledge that they will wake you at the first sign of trouble.

Turn to **344**.

### 195

The face of the worm is changing. It no longer resembles your brother Jen; it has taken on the haughty visage of the Demoness Shamath.

'Ha!' she snorts. 'How puny and insignificant you mortals are. There can be no sport for me in the easy slaying of your kind, for it is too easy. There is no challenge. Therefore I, Shamath, Mistress of the Gates of Darkness, shall devise one. I challenge you to a duel . . . a duel of intellect!'

The great worm-thing retreats towards the dais and the darkened walls of the cavern are suddenly illuminated by a thousand jets of flame, which roar from jets set into the smooth, glassy floor.

'Very well,' she says, fixing you with her supernatural eyes, 'let the combat begin.'

Turn to **189**.

**196**

As the Elder is hauling you off the bench, your robe gets snagged on a splinter and it rises up to reveal your boots and scabbard. The Elder is now angry and suspicious; he shouts at you, demanding to know how you came to be in possession of these items.

Pick a number from the *Random Number Table*.

If the number you have picked is *0–6*, turn to **190**.

If it is *7–9*, turn to **116**.

### 197

You speed across the room and lunge for the archer as he exits through the window. Your hand grabs hold of his breeches and you try to drag him back into the room, but he kicks free and leaves you clutching a fragment of cloth torn from the leg of his trousers.

If you wish to pursue the man on to the balcony, turn to **9**.

If you decide to let him go, you can leave the inn by the front door by turning to **231**.

### 198

You unshoulder your bow and draw an arrow with one swift and fluid movement. Then, as the beast's head crosses your line of sight, you release the shaft and send it whistling towards its gaping jaw.

Pick a number from the *Random Number Table*. If you possess Grand Weaponmastery with Bow, add 3 to the number you have picked.

If your total score is now *4* or less, turn to **48**.

If it is *5* or more, turn to **272**.

### 199

With your teeth clenched tightly against the fearful stench that is arising from the grave, you scrape away the remaining earth and stones and begin to search through the corpse's robes. There is little of value to be found here, nothing that the brigands have not already picked over. You are about to abandon this unpleasant task when suddenly you notice something protruding from the corpse's boot. It is a hexagonal token engraved with strange symbols, and it is made from the same black, metallic substance as the amulet given to you by President Kadharian.

You decide to keep this item. (Record this Special Item on your *Action Chart* as a Black Token which you carry in your pocket. If you already carry the maximum number of Special Items permissible, you must discard one in its favour.) Having satisfied your curiosity, you leave the gravesite and return to your horse, eager to continue your journey as quickly as you can.

Turn to **156**.

You stagger to your feet and shake your head to clear your blurred vision. The first thing you see when your sight returns to normal is the attacking longboat as it collides with the Vakovarian ship. With a deafening screech of twisting metal and shearing timbers, it shudders along the length of the starboard side, sending the brigands who are aboard cartwheeling helplessly across the deck. Grappling lines are cast and boarding planks lowered, and before the Vakovarians can recover, a screaming horde of red-robed acolytes are amongst them, slaying all without quarter.

On the quayside the Vakovarians are gripped by panic. Many flee to the ruins, but there is a core of battle-hardened ex-mercenaries who band together and attempt a counter-attack. Bloody fighting rages along the quayside as the acolytes try to recapture the three who are tied to the stone obelisk. The prisoners are eventually saved by a trio of acolyte Elders, each of whom is armed with a glowing wand that discharges an incinerating blast of energy against any brigand foolish enough to stand in their way. The Elders retreat to the long boat with the freed prisoners, but the fighting has started to spread beyond the quay. There is a sudden noise to your left, and when you turn to face it you see, two acolytes of Vashna racing along the street towards you with bloodied swords held ready to strike you down.

If you possess a Bow, and wish to use it, turn to **183**.

If you possess Kai-alchemy, and wish to use it, turn to **40**.

If you possess Magi-magic, and wish to use it, turn to **288**.

If you have none of these, or choose not to use them, turn to **140**.

### 201

You stare into the man's steel-blue eyes and, using your psychic skill, implant in his mind the suggestion that he should put his crossbow on the ground. You are hoping he will comply with your command so that you can attempt to get away, but then he says something which makes that idea redundant.

'You're no bandit,' he muses. 'No, by thunder, you look like a Sommlending to me.'

Turn to **13**.

## 202

President Kadharian is a tall, muscular man whose stern countenance reflects his unmistakably military background. He gives a formal salute, then he offers you his strong hand in friendship. You accept readily, without hesitation.

'Welcome, Grand Master,' he says, his jade-green eyes glinting warmly in the torchlit hall. 'I am deeply honoured that you have answered my call. I trust your journey to Helgor was not too difficult?'

'I encountered no problems that couldn't be overcome,' you reply.

'Good, good,' he says, and gives a knowing laugh. Then he bids you accompany him as he crosses the floor of the senate hall and pushes open the door to a smaller adjoining room.

'And now to the business in hand. I shall endeavour to explain the reasons why I felt it necessary to request your help, Grand Master.'

Turn to **100**.

## 203

Darkness descends as you ride down from the hill pass, but the twisting trail is kept illuminated by a spectacular host of twinkling lights which swoop and soar above the glimmering waters of the lake. It is a wondrous display but you are not deceived into

XI.  He offers you his strong hand in friendship.

thinking that all is well. There is a great and evil magic at work here; you can sense it.

You have ridden to within five kilometres of Vorn when you are forced to leave the trail and take cover. Ahead you see a group of Vakovarian bandits encamped on a bridge which carries the trail across a fast-flowing stream. Rather than risk a confrontation, you take cover in a wooded grove and spend a restless night waiting for the dawn. Due to the proximity of the enemy, you are unable to sleep – lose 3 ENDURANCE points.

To continue, turn to **339**.

## 204

Fear tightens its grip on your senses as you move slowly towards the arch. You are terrified by the thought of what might happen when you enter, but you dare not falter now. If you refuse to enter the arch, the acolytes of Vashna will know that you are not one of them.

If you possess the Dagger of Vashna, turn to **20**.
If you possess Helshezag, turn to **81**.
If you do not possess either of these Special Items, turn to **343**.

## 205

The ferocity of their attack leaves you sprawled on the floor of the cave, holding your aching head with both hands. Having encountered unexpected resistance, the phantoms veer away and vanish into the clouds. They have gone, but not for long. Within minutes they return with seven more of their ghostly brothers in train.

If you possess Kai-surge, and have reached the rank of Sun Lord, or higher, turn to **229**.

If you do not possess this Discipline, or if you have yet to attain this level of Kai rank, turn to **142**.

## 206

You have difficulty controlling the tremendous forces contained within the Deathstaff. Some of the Vortexi are able to seize upon this weakness and break away from the spinning cyclone to make good their attack.

Vortexi: COMBAT SKILL 44    ENDURANCE 30

For every level of Kai rank you have attained above that of Kai Grand Guardian, you may add 2 to your COMBAT SKILL for the duration of this fight. However, due to the insidious effect of the Deathstaff, you must reduce your ENDURANCE score by 3 prior to the start of this combat.

If you win the combat, turn to **46**.

## 207

The hut has long been deserted but it still offers you and your horse good protection against the elements. It is watertight and there is sufficient straw on the floor to feed your mount and keep you warm during the night.

Before you settle down to rest, unless you possess Grand Huntmastery you must eat a Meal or lose 3 ENDURANCE points.

Sheltered from the foul storm, you are able to get a good night's rest. You awake the following morning feeling invigorated: restore 3 ENDURANCE points.

To continue, turn to **285**.

## 208

Through a gap in the boulders you see a pack of eight ridge-backed jackals feeding on the carcass of a Durncrag scavenger, a vulture-like bird of prey. They are engrossed in their meal until they detect the scent of their most-favoured food: live horsemeat.

With another frenzied howl the wild jackals abandon the feathery carcass and come streaming through the gap in the boulders, drawn by the scent of your horse. They seem to know that he is in a weakened state and this fuels their fury. Your horse takes fright and tries to pull away, his hooves flailing the air perilously close to your skull, and as the first of the jackals make its attack, you find yourself struggling to hold on to the reins with one hand and fight off the jackals with the other.

Vorndarol jackals:
COMBAT SKILL 42    ENDURANCE 38

Unless you possess Grand Weaponmastery and have reached the rank of Sun Knight, or higher, you must reduce your COMBAT SKILL by 5 for the duration of this combat.

You may evade combat after four rounds, by turning to **222**.
If you win this fight, turn to **347**.

## 209

You gallop down the muddy track towards a cleft in the gulley which is protected by the overhanging ledge. Here you command Bracer to halt, but he does not respond as you would wish. He paws at the ground and refuses to stand still. You feel sure that the lightning flashes, the burning trees, and the deafening cracks of thunder are the reasons why he is so unsettled. In an attempt to calm him down, you draw on your innate Kai skill of animal kinship. In doing so you suddenly discover the real reason why he is so agitated.

Turn to **319**.

**210**

You pull your horse back from the body of the dead corvayl and gallop away in case there are others of its kind lurking nearby. Beyond the plateau, the trail descends steeply towards a thick pine wood. Milky-white pools of water punctuate this section of the track, some deceptively deep, making the descent difficult and tiring. By the time you reach the wood your horse is in need of rest.

You dismount to take the weight off his back, and as you gather his reins together you notice that the flap of your Backpack is undone. On checking the contents you discover that one of your possessions is missing. (Erase the second item on your list of Backpack Items. If you have only one item on your list, erase that one instead.)

As soon as your horse is rested, you remount him and set off through the pine wood heading east.

Turn to **300**.

## 211

Your mastery of the Kai camouflage skills makes you virtually undetectable. The Vakovarians search the inn thoroughly but they fail to find you, even though one passes so close that he treads on your foot.

You wait until they have gone, then you leave the inn and make your way down through the ruins towards the lake, taking care to avoid those other Vakovarians who are out looting. The burnt-out shell of a meeting hall offers you an unobstructed view of the quay and its flagstoned square. You hide here, invisible among the charred roof timbers, and watch as a curious scene unfolds on the quayside outside.

Turn to **163**.

## 212

You focus on the brigand leader as you whisper the words of the Brotherhood spell 'Mind Charm'. You will him to send away his henchmen and, when he is alone, you close in on him from behind without making a sound.

Turn to **119**.

## 213

You level the Deathstaff at the Arch Druid, and say, 'This is the key to the resurrection of Vashna; without it your Demoness will be powerless to summon him.'

Cadak laughs sneeringly at your words. 'And how long do you think you will keep it from her, Kai lord? Do you think that the Demoness Shamath will have difficulty taking it from you? No, she will not. You are doomed, Lone Wolf. Why don't you admit it? You were doomed the moment you returned from the great arch.'

Your hatred for the evil druid wells up and you suddenly feel a tingling sensation engulf your hands. Your emotion has activated the power of the Deathstaff and, without warning, a swirling cone of grey vapour emerges from its tip and coils towards Cadak. He yelps with shocked surprise and raises his staff to fend off the attack. He is successful, but at great cost to his magical stamina.

You, too, feel the draining effect of this accursed staff (lose 7 ENDURANCE points) and your Kai senses scream a warning not to use it again in combat for fear of the consequences. Next time you could lose more than ENDURANCE points – you could lose your soul!

Turn to **252**.

## 214

You focus your power on a small pile of rocks lying at the edge of an outcrop which overhangs the boulder. The vibrations that you set up dislodge the rocks and make them cascade on to the boulder beneath. Suddenly, there is a cry of alarm and a man springs up from behind the boulder, shielding his head with both arms as he scurries out in the open to avoid the deluge. He is a grey-bearded man, clad in furs and armed with an expensive-looking cross-bow which is slung by a leather strap around his shoulder. By his looks you judge him to be a hunter, not a brigand.

Coughing and spitting dust, he wipes his face with his hairy hands then turns to look in your direction. You sense that he is about to reach for his crossbow, but when you raise your hand in a show of friendship, he pauses and narrows his eyes, as if he is trying to get a clearer look at you.

'You're no Vakovarian,' he muses. 'No, by thunder, you look like a Sommlending to me.'

Chuckling under his breath, he makes his way down the slope and comes walking towards you with a broad smile on his weather-beaten face.

Turn to **340**.

## 215

A wave of panic sweeps through the crowded inn. Women shriek hysterically and gruff voices shout in anger and confusion, demanding Smudd's killer be found. You back away from the alcove and, as you turn towards the counter, you catch a glimpse of a

XII.   You catch a glimpse of a figure running along the
gallery.

figure running along the gallery which overlooks the taproom floor. He is clad from head to toe in a close-fitting black tunic and he is carrying a bow. You watch helplessly as he disappears through a door which leads off the gallery.

If you wish to climb an adjoining staircase and give chase, turn to **259**.

If you choose to leave the inn by the front door, turn to **56**.

### 216

The Demoness laughs with disdain at your inability to answer her riddle. She denounces you as unworthy of her presence and says that, although she will derive little pleasure from it, she is now going to have to kill you.

Demoness Shamath (in the guise of Gnekasha the Worm-thrall): COMBAT SKILL 55    ENDURANCE 42

If you win this combat, turn to **148**.

### 217

You sheathe your weapon and hold out your open palms to show that you have no intention of harming them. They seem to respond to this gesture and they allow you to approach and examine their sickly child. You tell them that you can help their son and, using your innate healing skills, you place your hands upon the boy's chest and let your Kai power flow through into his fever-wracked body. Within a few moments he stirs to consciousness and gives a healthy cry; you have saved his life.

Turn to **277**.

## 218

Beyond the perimeter of the settlement the path steadily gets steeper as it ascends into the hills. The torch-bearing line of acolytes illuminates the rocky landscape with flickering shadows as slowly they zigzag their way eastwards. Another storm is brewing; the eastern sky is alive with electrical activity and thunder booms beyond the horizon. Your ears pop as the air pressure fluctuates wildly and the howl of the wind seems to be growing ever louder. Then you notice something strange. Your torch does not seem to be affected by the storm; it is burning as smoothly as if you were in an enclosed room. You glance over your shoulder and see that the same is true of every other torch. It is as if the procession is being protected from the outside elements by an invisible tunnel.

Two kilometres from the settlement you pass a group of acolyte youths, all in their early teens, who are calling encouragement, chanting, and waving the line onwards. Then the path bends and you see a wayside altar and a large marble trough filled with stagnant green water. As they file past, every acolyte dips his right hand into the trough and touches it to his heart.

If you possess a Black Token, turn to **349**.

If you do not possess this Special Item, turn to **121**.

## 219

You shuffle along the bench, hoping that this will appease the Elder, but it merely serves to anger him. He shouts at you and, thinking that you are being deliberately insubordinate, he grabs your robe in both hands and pulls you roughly to your feet.

If you possess a Runic Disc, turn to **255**.
If you do not possess this Special Item, turn to **196**.

### 220

Immediately you recognize the man: he is Gwynian, the Sage of Varetta.

'Welcome, Grand Master. It has been a long time since we last met. Come, step into my humble abode. The time has come once more for us to discuss the future.'

Turn to **178**.

### 221

Your Kai mastery informs you that this creature is telling the truth. You also sense that she is not human, she is a supernatural creature, not of your world or this. You scan her mind but it is impossible for you to penetrate her psychic defences. She seems to possess contradictory qualities; she is both good and evil.

Turn to **286**.

### 222

You leap into the saddle and steer your terrified horse away from the frenzied jackals. Bloodied in combat, they stand off just long enough for you to urge your horse to the gallop and get away along the shore. With the help of your Kai mastery, he crosses the difficult terrain with agility, despite his fatigue, and soon reaches firmer ground where he is able to increase his pace and escape from the howling pack.

The jackals command the shore and you are forced to retrace your steps all the way back to the fork in the trail and take the other path that leads into the foothills. By the time you arrive here, you are tired and very hungry. Unless you possess Grand Hunt-mastery, you must eat 1 Meal or lose 3 ENDURANCE points.

To continue, turn to **61**.

## 223

Your keen Kai senses detect the warm scent of horse flesh on the air, mingling with the sharp tang of the surrounding pine trees. Hopeful that it is Bracer, escaped from the brigands and come to find you, you push through the densely-packed trees until you stumble upon a clearing. Here you discover that it is not Bracer after all; you have found the brigands' horses.

They are unguarded and you cannot sense their owners close by, but even so you take every care not to startle them. Silently you untether one of the stallions and lead him away from the rest of the horses, along a trail which is covered with fresh tracks, and soon you come to a wider trail which winds away to the north. Here you mount the horse and set off along this rocky trail, but you have gone little more than half a mile when you smell something that makes you rein your new horse to a halt. From a wooded gulley away to your right you detect the scent of death being carried on the afternoon breeze.

If you wish to investigate the wooded gulley, turn to **342**.

If you choose to avoid it and ride on, turn to **156**.

## 224

You intensify your vision and focus upon the figure who commands the crystal dais. Shock freezes your spine when you recognize at once the face and flowing platinum hair of Arch Druid Cadak, ruler of Mogaruith, the usurper lord of Kaag. He has grown strong since your last fateful encounter, and now it seems that he is poised to fulfil the Dark God Naar's lust for vengeance by releasing Vashna and his hordes from the depths of the Maakengorge.

You take your place among the throng who are kneeling before the dais, and hear Cadak's voice ring out above the howling storm.

'I summon forth from the Vortex of the Planes the Deliverer of Vashna, Mighty Lord of Darkness,

Prince of the Legions of the Restless Dead. Come to us. Come to us now and fulfil our destiny. We, the worthy, now prove our faith in the undying power of Vashna.'

With these words, the acolytes utter a chilling cry of affirmation and rise to their feet. By rank they follow the Elders in single file towards a smaller, shimmering metallic arch which stands to one side of the crystal dais, almost obscured by the glare of the larger one. One by one they file through this archway, under the watchful gaze of Cadak, and then return to their places where they kneel and pray.

As you approach the smaller arch, you sense a curtain of power drawn across it. Anxiously you pray to the Gods Kai and Ishir to protect you as you prepare to pass through this invisible barrier.

If you possess the Sommerswerd, turn to **166**.
If you do not possess this Special Item, turn to **204**.

## 225

You wrench the Deathstaff from the dais and sag beneath its unnatural weight. The moment you raise it into the air, the Demoness spins around to stare at you, sending her attendants flying in all directions. She screams with unholy anger and the noise of her wrath lifts you bodily and sends you skidding across the floor.

Desperately you fight to maintain your grip on the Deathstaff as the furious Shamath gets to her feet. She comes striding towards you, bolts of energy darting from her fingertips to rip open the ground as you stumble away towards the yawning black tunnel. The deafening shriek of Shamath's voice rings in your ears as you clutch the Deathstaff to your chest and leap head first into the oblivion of the shadow gate.

Turn to **270**.

## 226

You tether your horse's reins to a peg beside the door and step into the welcoming warmth of the furrier's shop. Immediately you are assailed by the greasy stench of the furs which fill this emporium. They hang in rows from ornate brass hooks driven into the wooden walls and ceiling rafters, sorted by size and type. Three young men, all strikingly similar in looks, are busy trimming wolf pelts at a work bench. Behind the counter stands a grey-haired old woman with a straight back and clear, milky-white skin. She smiles and asks if you wish to buy or sell furs.

'Neither, madam,' you reply, politely, 'I'm trying to find my way to an inn called the Crooked Sage.'

'Oh, you are, are you?' she mumbles, disappointedly, her welcoming smile fading as she abandons hopes of striking up a deal with you. Then her smile returns and she says, 'Well, sir, I'll be glad to tell you . . . but only if you buy something first. If you won't buy any of my furs, then I'll sell you the information you want for five Gold Crowns. What do you say?'

Without replying, you step away from the counter and look up. On a square of black slate hanging

XIII.   She smiles and asks you if you wish to buy or sell furs.

above the old woman's head are chalked the following items and prices:

| | |
|---|---|
| Coney-skin mitts | 5 Gold Crowns a pair |
| Wolfskin cloaks | 12 Gold Crowns each |
| Wildcat pelts | 12 Gold Crowns each |
| Bearskin cloaks | 16 Gold Crowns each |
| White wolf pelts | 18 Gold Crowns each |
| Kalkoth hides | 20 Gold Crowns each |
| Black corvayl cloaks | 35 Gold Crowns each |

All of the above furs are Backpack Items. If you wish to purchase any (or should you decide to pay 5 Gold Crowns for directions to the Crooked Sage), deduct the appropriate amount of Gold Crowns and adjust your *Action Chart* accordingly. Then, turn to **174**.

If you decide not to buy any furs, or pay for the information, turn instead to **77**.

### 227

The arrow streaks into the bushes and you hear it shatter against the rocks behind. Then you hear the faint scrape of leather on stone, above and to the side. You turn to look and a man's voice growls, 'Don't move!'

Standing between two boulders away to your left is a grey-bearded man, clad in furs clutching a loaded crossbow. The weapon is pointing directly at your heart.

If you possess the Discipline of Telegnosis, and wish to use it, turn to **201**.

If you do not possess this skill, or choose not to use it, turn to **280**.

## 228

'Ha! I know you, intruder,' yells Cadak, maniacally, 'You are Lone Wolf, the doomed hero of a doomed realm. You are a fool to come here, Kai lord. Your powers are no match for those of Naar, the King of the Darkness.'

With this he turns to the acolytes and throws up his hands triumphantly.

'This night we shall celebrate a double victory, my brethren. The resurrection of Lord Vashna and the destruction of Grand Master Lone Wolf!'

The acolytes scream their approval, but their cheer is drowned by the ever-increasing noise of the storm. Then you see that the storm itself is changing. A huge vortex of whirling cloud is descending from the heavens, a tornado whose deadly funnel is reaching down towards you. Then the tip of the roaring plume touches the ground at your feet and, with a terrifying suddenness, you are torn from the energy curtain and sent hurtling through the air towards the dark centre of the towering arch.

Turn to **60**.

## 229

You open the depths of your mind and summon forth a glowing ball of Kai energy which you project at the leading phantom. This fiery ball of psychic power rips into the creature's ghostly form and causes it to shriek with agony. Your Kai blast has wounded this entity, but it has not stopped its attack. It gathers itself and swoops down upon you, like a hungry vulture descending on a corpse.

Vortexi (weakened by Kai blast):
COMBAT SKILL 40    ENDURANCE 22

For every level of Kai rank you have attained above that of Kai Grand Guardian, you may add 2 to your COMBAT SKILL for the duration of this fight. If you possess the Sommerswerd, add 5 to your ENDURANCE points score.

If you win the combat, turn to **159**.

### 230

A kilometre beyond the cove the shoreline trail becomes littered with boulders and huge mounds of muddy earth. It is the debris of landslides from the surrounding hills, a consequence of the violent storms. It soon becomes impossible to continue on horseback and you are forced to dismount and make your way on foot, with your horse trailing behind you.

During this difficult trek an icy squall arises, driven by a gale-force wind which whips the shoreline mercilessly. Your innate skills of Nexus protect you from the cold, but your horse is not so lucky. You know that you must find shelter from this bitter wintery squall, and quickly, if he is to survive.

As you reach the top of a rocky mound, you see below you a cluster of huge boulders grouped in a horseshoe circle near the lake's edge; they promise good protection from the squall.

If you possess Grand Pathsmanship, turn to **302**.
If you do not possess this Discipline, turn to **168**.

## 231

The gamblers are enraged that their privacy has been invaded. They crowd in on you, demanding an explanation, but you push them aside and leave the room without uttering a word. At the bottom of the gallery stairs you are met by an excited throng of people, still shocked and angered by Smudd's murder. Some openly blame you and attempt to stop you from leaving. By the time you have forced your way across the taproom to the doors of the inn, your face is bleeding and your body is bruised from their kicks and punches.

You stumble out into the street and, as you turn towards the stables to go and retrieve your horse, your eagle eyes catch a glimpse of movement on a second storey balcony. It is the archer you saw a few minutes ago, the man in black who fled from the gallery. With bated breath you watch as he climbs on to the balcony rail and leaps across the narrow street on to the roof of the building opposite.

Turn to **274**.

## 232

Terror grips your heart as you feel yourself sinking into the cavern floor. Your feet have completely disappeared from sight when suddenly the sinking sensation stops . . . but the terror goes on. Suddenly you hear a hideous squeaking sound high above your head. You look up into the vaulted ceiling and gasp with dread as a writhing cloud of crypt spawn come plummeting down towards your face.

Crypt spawn: COMBAT SKILL 43    ENDURANCE 35

Reduce your COMBAT SKILL by 4 for the duration of this fight due to your immobility.

If you win the combat, turn to **79**.

## 233

Soon the temperature begins to drop and the great grey wall of fog condenses and falls as rain. This rain freezes and you quickly find yourself surrounded by a wall of glittering ice which stretches like a range of jagged glass mountains from horizon to horizon.

In the distance you see a dim light flickering and twinkling at the heart of these ice mountains. You strike out towards it, across the frost-encrusted ground, and find yourself covering the distance far quicker than would ever be possible on Magnamund. A kilometre slips by at a single step and the surrounding terrain becomes impossible to focus on.

Suspecting that you are the victim of some powerful illusion, you stride up to the flickering ice wall and thrust your hand against it. Effortlessly, your palm sinks into the glassy blue surface and you fall headlong into the icy mountainside.

Turn to **44**.

## 234

You remove the amulet from your pocket and hand it to the old sage.

'President Kadharian gave me this. It was found on the shore of Lake Vorndarol, near the ruins of Vorn, by a rogue who went by the name of Smudd. I tracked him to a tavern in Helgor but he was assassinated before he could tell me anything more about it. Can you?'

Gwynian holds the amulet close to his myopic eyes and examines the engravings with great care. After a short while he says.

'It is a seal. It's an amulet of fealty worn by the acolytes of Vashna,' he says sadly. 'It would seem to confirm our fears. I have seen amulets such as this before, but none crafted from such a metal. This is a metal not of this world.'

Gwynian hands back the amulet and you return it to your pocket.

Turn to **45**.

## 235

Your first attempt at deciphering the secret of the crystal dais was not successful and a new sequence of numbers materializes upon the surface of the upper tier.

This time the sequence appears to be harder. Now you will need to bring to bear all your Kai skill and intelligence if you are to break the code and close the shadow gate in time. Or will you be defeated by your old enemy, Arch Druid Cadak, even after his death?

Study the following grid of numbers carefully. When you think you know the missing number, turn to the entry which bears the same number as your answer.

| 23 | 41 | 55 | 88 | 31 |
|----|----|----|----|----|
| 86 | 68 |    | 129 | 135 |
| 141 | 192 | 220 | 216 | 337 |

If you cannot solve the problem, turn to **141**.

## 236

A ball of lightning comes hurtling towards your head. Desperately, you pull your horse away to avoid being hit, but the fiery meteor changes course in mid-flight as if guided by an unseen hand. Instinctively, you draw your weapon and raise it to defend yourself from the onrushing ball of energy, suspecting it to be a spectral enemy in disguise. Then, with a blinding flash, it impacts upon your weapon and you are hurled from the saddle amidst a shower of glowing sparks.

> If the weapon you are wielding is a Bow or a Quarterstaff, turn to **308**.
> If you are wielding any other type of weapon, turn to **131**.

### 237

Using your advanced Kai mastery you can tell that, along with the heat, the token is giving off intense ultraviolet radiation. It is a cursed relic which has been activated by its proximity to the pool of stagnant water. The closer you get to the pool, the hotter and more reactive the relic becomes. Another few steps and it will explode. Knowing this, you fumble to retrieve it from the smoking pocket of your tunic, and hurl it away.

Pick a number from the *Random Number Table*.

> If the number you have picked is *0–1*, turn to **96**.
> If it is *2–9*, turn to **316**.

### 238

'Who found this amulet?' you ask.

'A rogue, one who goes by the name of Smudd,' answers Kadharian. 'A patrol found him in the mountains close by the River Storn, a few days after the second troop went missing. When he couldn't give a good reason for being there, they arrested him and brought him back to Helgor for *questioning*.'

Kadharian's emphasis on the word 'questioning'

leaves you in no doubt that Smudd's interrogation probably involved some degree of torture.

'Where is he now?' you ask. 'I'd like to, er, question him myself.'

'He's in Helgor. He stays at the Crooked Sage, an inn in the north quarter of the city. I'd willingly send a detachment of Palace Guards to fetch him here but that quarter of Helgor is rife with villians. Word would be sure to get out and he'd go to ground. My men would never find him. No, I'm afraid the only likely way you'll get to speak to Smudd is by going to the Crooked Sage in person.'

'Very well, President,' you reply, 'then that is exactly what I shall do.'

Turn to **84**.

Turn to **84**.

### 239

'We have an intruder in our midst,' screams Cadak. You fight the paralysing effect of the current and, for a moment, its effect weakens. Then the crimson current intensifies anew, numbing your limbs with its insidious effect.

'Ha! I know you, intruder,' yells Cadak, maniacally, 'You are Lone Wolf, the doomed hero of a doomed realm. You are a fool to come here, Kai lord. Your powers are no match for those of Naar, the King of the Darkness.'

With this he turns to the acolytes and throws up his hands triumphantly. 'This night we shall celebrate a double victory, my brethren. The resurrection of Lord Vashna and the destruction of Grand Master Lone Wolf!'

The acolytes scream their approval, but their cheer is drowned by the ever-increasing noise of the storm. Then you see that the storm itself is changing. A huge vortex of whirling cloud is descending from the heavens, a tornado whose deadly funnel is reaching down towards you. Then the tip of the roaring plume touches the ground at your feet and, with a terrifying suddenness, you are torn from the energy curtain and sent hurtling through the air towards the dark centre of the towering arch.

Turn to **60**.

### 240

As the last automaton drops at your feet, you sheathe your weapon and race towards the dais. During your fight, the Demoness was putting on an armoured breastplate of varnished black steel and was otherwise distracted. But she saw you slay the last of her automatons and now she is aware of your plan. She has no intention of allowing you anywhere near the dais or the Deathstaff.

If you possess Kai-alchemy, turn to **57**.
If you do not possess this Grand Master Discipline, turn to **282**.

### 241

Hurriedly you leave the trail, steering Bracer through the undergrowth towards the cover of a dense pine copse. Here, you quickly dismount and tie his reins to a tree before going forward to see what you can find.

You soon discover that a gang of brigands are lying in ambush, well hidden among the boulders that line

XIV. You soon discover that a gang of brigands are lying
in ambush.

both sides of the trail. Your Kai hunting skills enable you to circle around and get behind them without being seen and, from a high vantage point among the boulders, you observe their leader and three of his henchmen hiding behind the bough of a fallen tree.

If you possess a Bow and wish to fire an arrow at the brigand leader, turn to **304**.

If you possess Kai-alchemy and wish to use the spell of 'Mind Charm', turn to **212**.

If you decide to wait and observe the brigands a little longer , turn to **98**.

### 242

Slowly the cavern begins to darken and the towering body of the Demoness shimmers and changes into a new and totally repugnant form: she has taken on the guise of a huge crawling worm. Her slimy flanks are studded with a multitude of tiny tendrils, and her head is equipped with a sphincter-like maw which drips loathsome green saliva. She slithers closer and, in the half-light, you catch sight of her ghastly face. It is like that of an infant, wholly black, save for the eyes which are aglow with a hellish red fire.

The worm-thing rears up and, as the head sweeps past your eyes a second time, you suddenly recognize the facial features and a paralysing blast of psychic shock rips through your mind. It has the face of your long-dead brother Jen.

If you possess Kai-screen, turn to **68**.

If you do not possess mastery of this Discipline, turn to **101**.

## 243

You turn your head slightly and see a pair of sandalled feet standing on the deck by your side. They belong to the Elder whom you almost collided with when you jumped aboard the longboat. He repeats his command and this time, aided by your Kai mastery, you understand what he says. He is commanding you to get up and go forward to the bow and help with the carrying of some wounded acolytes to the stern.

You nod to signify you acknowledge his order yet you do not raise your head — to do so would risk him seeing your face. Unfortunately, as you rise from the bench, your robe gets snagged on a splinter and is pulled up to reveal your boots and scabbard. The Elder becomes suspicious and he demands to know how you came to be in possession of these items.

If you possess a Runic Disc, turn to **55**.
If you wish to say that you took them from a dead Vakovarian during the battle at the quay, turn to **82**.
If you choose to pretend that you did not hear him, turn to **22**.

## 244

You have ridden less than twenty metres when a sudden gust of wind thins out the cloying fog, revealing the dark entrance to an alleyway off to your right.

If you wish to explore this alley, turn to **33**.
If you decide to ignore it and continue on your way along this street, turn to **147**.

## 245

As you hurry towards the end of the procession, an Elder steps out from behind a boulder and grabs you by the shoulder, commanding you to halt. Then you feel a tingling sensation, as if a horde of spiders were crawling in a line from your shoulder to the nape of your neck; the Elder has psychic abilities and he is attempting to probe your mind.

If you possess Kai-screen, turn to **126**.
If you do not possess this Grand Master Discipline, turn to **74**.

## 246

A shudder runs through the dais and fingers of green electrical fire shoot from the tip of the Deathstaff into the ground below. There is a moment of dreadful silence when even the storm and the rain abate, then the air shakes with a terrific implosion as the great shimmering arch collapses inwards and slowly disintegrates. Sparkling sheets of energy buckle and fuse as segments of the arch fall to the ground, crushing everything beneath, rock and man. For an instant you catch a glimpse of a huge booted foot stepping through a silvery sheet of energy and you tremble at the thought of what will happen next, for you recognize only too well to whom the foot belongs. But in the very next instant the keystone of the arch falls away and, with a grating cry of tortured rock, the whole edifice comes crashing to the ground.

Then, as if from nowhere, a raging whirlwind arises in mid-air, at the centre of where the arch stood. This whirling vortex quickly builds in power until it is sucking everything into its spinning black core. Screaming acolytes tumble past and disappear into its maw as you desperately hang on to the dais to stop yourself from being sucked to your doom.

Pick a number from the *Random Number Table*.

If your current ENDURANCE points score is 14 or higher, add 2 to the number you picked.

If your current ENDURANCE points score is 13 or lower, deduct 1 from the number you picked.

If you possess Kai-alchemy, and have attained the Kai rank of Sun Knight, add 5 to the number you picked.

If your total score is now 4 or less, turn to **313**. If it is 5 or more, turn to **350**.

## 247

When you sense it is safe to do so, you stop to catch your breath and examine the contents of the satchel, which you empty out on to the ground. It contains the following items:

80 Gold Crowns
Enough food for 3 Meals
Quiver (containing 3 arrows)
Bottle of Wine
Spyglass
Ruby Ring

If you wish to keep any of the above, remember to adjust your *Action Chart* accordingly.

The area is alive with bandits and you are forced to

flee northwards, away from the place where you left Bracer tethered to a tree. You are anxious for his safety and mindful that there are still many kilometres to be covered before you reach Lake Vorndarol, but you dare not turn back for him. Then you hear something that makes you halt in your tracks: it is the sound of a horse whinnying.

Turn to **223**.

### 248

Having decided not to approach the circle of boulders, the only option left to you is to turn back to the fork in the trail and take the other path that leads into the foothills. By the time you arrive there, you are tired and very hungry. Unless you possess Grand Huntmastery, you must eat a Meal or lose 3 ENDURANCE points.

To continue, turn to **61**.

### 249

You focus your power of animal control on the leader of this predatory flock and will him to abandon his attack. The speed of his descent is making it difficult for you to target him, but your persistence and your Kai skills overcome this. At the last moment the ugly black bird banks away, cawing frantically, and the remainder of his flock follow suit without pressing home their attack. You watch with grim satisfaction as the flock return to the mountains, cawing with frustration, their hunger unsatiated.

You manage to regain control of the raft and, at length, you reach the far side of the river and disembark safely. A stony trail runs along the bank, heading north, and you follow it with high hopes of reaching Lake Vorndarol before sunset. All day the sun blazes supreme in a cloudless sky and waves of heat create a shimmering, distorted view of the trail ahead. The distant horizon is streaked with myriad colours and the dry air crackles with electricity, a legacy of last night's violent storm. Late in the afternoon you come to the ruins of an ancient settlement and stop here to allow your horse to rest awhile in the shade.

If you possess Grand Pathsmanship, turn to **102**.
If you do not possess this Discipline, turn to **260**.

## 250

For three kilometres you trek stolidly through the hills towards a deep magenta glow that is bathing the horizon. Then, as you round a knoll of rock, shaped like an accusing skeletal finger, you are confronted by a spectacle which leaves you staring openmouthed with awe and horror.

An expanse of dead land, littered with cracked and shattered rocks, slopes down to the edge of an immense chasm that stretches more than a kilometre from rim to rim. It is the Maakengorge. Hordes of screeching vortexi ride a violent electrical storm which rages in the clouds above this vast abyss, and the earth shudders in echoing response to the booming thunder. Near the rim of the chasm there stands a towering arch, hewn of stone, that shimmers with such a supernatural brilliance that you cannot fully focus upon it. Peering closer you see before the arch an elaborate, multi-tiered dais constructed entirely of crystal. Around it kneel hundreds of acolytes who

XV. You follow the procession as it winds its way towards the dais.

are chanting devoutly. Their dreary voices add to the
dreadful noise.

You follow the procession as it winds its way towards
the dais and soon you see that a solitary figure is
standing upon its uppermost tier. He faces the shimmering arch, his hands outstretched, and with every
movement of his fingers there is a subtle shift in the
spectrum of colours within the angry clouds above.
It is as if he is manipulating the storm as a conductor
would an orchestra. With a grand sweep of his arms
he calms the turbulent sky, then he turns to face his
kneeling congregation.

If you have ever been to Kaag or Mogaruith, turn
to **224**.

If you have never been to these city-fortresses,
turn to **295**.

# 251

The tip of your arrow clips the man's calf and you
hear him yelp with pain. But the wound is superficial
and it does not prevent him from making his escape
out on to the balcony.

With weapon in hand, you climb out of the window.
You are expecting the archer to attack you the
moment you appear but the balcony is deserted: he
has disappeared. Then your keen eyes notice fresh
bloodstains on the balcony rail and you catch a
glimpse of movement on the roof of the building
opposite. It is the archer. Despite his wounded leg he
has leapt across the narrow street and is now making
his escape across the rooftops of the north quarter.

With the grace of a panther you spring on to the

balcony rail and leap across to the roof opposite. Without breaking your stride, you set off after the fleeing assassin and pursue him to the edge of a flat-topped warehouse at the end of Tavern Lane. Here a plank of wood has been laid down to span the gap of fifteen metres to the rooftop opposite. The man limps across the plank, then kicks it away to prevent you from following him.

If you are determined to follow him and wish to try to leap across the gap, turn to **42**.

If you do not wish to make the jump, turn to **191**.

### 252

You sense that Cadak is playing for time. It is his wish to keep you imprisoned within this umbrella of light until the Demoness Shamath arrives. Then you recall the words of the young girl whom you encountered in the cavern — *'Be brave, Grand Master. But most of all — be swift!'*

If you possess Kai-alchemy and wish to use it, turn to **123**.

If you possess Kai-surge and wish to use it, turn to **267**.

If you possess neither of these skills, or if you choose not to use them, turn to **54**.

### 253

You use your advanced healing skills to staunch the flow of blood from your gashed neck and to mend the torn tissue. Within a few moments the pain subsides, and sufficient strength returns to your aching limbs to enable you to break from cover and run after your horse.

You enter the dense pine copse to find Bracer standing among the trees, whinnying nervously. You calm him down and secure his reins to a branch, then you go back and try to catch a glimpse of your attackers. As you reach the edge of the trees you have no difficulty seeing them: a dozen brigands, brandishing crossbows and swords, are rushing through the knee-high undergrowth towards your hiding place.

If you possess a Bow and wish to use it, turn to **330**.

If you do not, turn to **136**.

You draw an arrow and take aim in the direction you can hear the beast approaching. It sounds as if it is no more than twenty metres away when you release the straining bowstring and send the arrow streaking into the fog. The shaft has travelled barely a few metres when it ignites with a flash and is instantly transformed into a line of glowing splinters which float away on the mist.

As soon as the arrow passed beyond the perimeter of the protection of your Platimun Amulet, it was subjected to the true temperature of this domain, a temperature which reduced it to glowing embers in less than a second.

Suddenly, with a deafening roar, the unseen beast is upon you. You drop your bow and unsheathe your weapon as it tries to rake you unmercifully with fang and claw.

Zarthyn: COMBAT SKILL 48    ENDURANCE 50

If you win this combat, turn to **90**.

### 255

The runic disc that you found in Helgor falls from your pocket as the Elder hauls you roughly off the bench. It bounces off the deck and comes to rest on his foot. He releases his grip on your robe and stoops to pick it up, thinking that it is booty you have looted from Vorn. But his temper quickly cools when he recognizes it to be the mark of the Guild of Rhem, the most feared brotherhood of assassins in all of northern Magnamund. He is aware that some guild assassins have been employed as agents to carry out missions for the acolytes, and he assumes at once that you are such an agent.

Nervously he returns the disc to you. Then, without further word, he backs away a few paces, bows his head, and leaves to attend to other matters at the prow of the boat. Those seated around you have now become uncomfortably curious. To avoid their attentions, you get up and move to the stern where a score of acolytes are kneeling in prayer.

Turn to **124**.

### 256

Your advanced Kai skills and the mud make it easy for you to tell that these tracks were made by humans travelling on foot. You count eight different pairs of footprints: six made by sandalled feet, and two by heavy hobnailed boots. The tracks are two days old and they are all heading in a north-easterly direction.

Turn to **67**.

## 257

You raise your weapon and bring your horse about to face this fearsome beast's attack. The instant he sees the creature he panics and rears up on his hind legs, neighing with fright, his hooves scrabbling frantically at the air. You bring him under control using your innate Kai skills, but in doing so your attention is diverted from the attacking beast as it moves in and swipes at you with its clawed paw.

Black corvayl: COMBAT SKILL 46    ENDURANCE 58

Reduce your COMBAT SKILL by 10 for the first round of this fight only.

If you win the combat, turn to **210**.

## 258

Your psychic defences hold fast and the Elder learns nothing from his attempt to read your mind. Rather than admit to failure, he curses and denounces you as an empty-headed cretin.

With a growl of disdain, he orders you to rejoin the end of the procession and pushes you out of his way as he strides back to rally those acolytes who are fleeing down the path.

Turn to **250**.

## 259

You race up the staircase and kick open the door through which the black-clad archer disappeared. Inside, you discover a group of gamblers standing at a circular table with playing cards in their hands. They have all risen from their seats to look at something on the far side of the room. When you follow their gaze, you see it is the archer; he is climbing through an open window on to a balcony outside.

If you possess a Bow and wish to use it, turn to **301**.

If you do not, turn to **197**.

**260**

You leave the ancient settlement and continue your ride along the sun-baked river trail. As dusk approaches, you keep a weather eye open for the signs of a storm. Clouds are rapidly forming over the mountains to the east, and the metallic smell of ozone is strong on the evening breeze.

In the middle distance you see a large herd of Vythaz. These timid, goat-like mountain animals are rarely seen at this time of the year, yet here are more than two hundred of them drinking at the river's edge. You sense that they are nervous and confused; the eerie weather has disrupted their natural migratory instincts and they have descended to the river a season earlier than is usual.

Suddenly, there is a flash of lightning and a mighty clap of thunder explodes in the sky overhead. The herd scatter in all directions, terrified by the noise. Then an incredible ball of light shoots down from the heavens and hits the trail, scattering stones like shrapnel and leaving a huge, smoking crater in its wake. You pull your horse off the trail and run with the fleeing Vythaz herd as more of the lightning balls streak down from the stormy sky.

If you possess the Sommerswerd, turn to **321**.
If you do not possess this Special Item, turn to **236**.

## 261

The blazing cavern walls grow dim, and shimmering waves of the crimson light begin to sweep across the floor towards the crystal dais. Suddenly Shamath reappears in her female form at the base of the dais. In front of her booted legs there stand a dozen powerful warriors, armoured and helmeted as if for war, but their stern faces have no eyes and their mouths have no lips. Behind her, a score of new attendants emerge from the shadows carrying large pieces of shiny black armour. She begins to strap this armour to her limbs and, by the sluggishness of her movements, you can tell that she must have been weakened by your earlier conflict.

XVI. Suddenly Shamath appears in her female form at the base of the dais.

With a single word she commands the warriors to attack you. They raise their short swords and come marching slowly forwards, their movements stiff and machine-like. Beyond their advancing line you catch sight of the Deathstaff still lying near the base of the dais, and a bold plan springs to mind. If you could evade the oncoming line of automatons, you could reach the dais. Then you would be able to take the Deathstaff and enter the shadow gate before Shamath recovers her strength.

Turn to **171**.

### 262

Closer examination of the amulet reveals a wealth of detailed engravings which depict a chilling scene. They portray clearly the rising of Darklord Vashna and his minions from the depths of the Maaken-gorge. Your Kai skill reveals to you that this amulet once possessed a powerful charge that could have killed anyone who touched it. That charge is spent, but you can still detect the faint, lingering aura of the evil being who crafted this artefact.

Turn to **238**.

### 263

Guided by your Kai instincts, you raise the Deathstaff and whirl it around your head — once, twice, three times . . .

An ominous hum radiates from its haft. There is a crackle of static electricity and the damp air seethes with restrained, undischarged power. A thread of mist issues from the staff's tip and builds rapidly into a spinning cyclone that ensnares the vortexi and prevents them from reaching you. In desperation, you sense them pooling their immense psychic energies in an attempt to break out of this whirling prison and attack you.

Pick a number from the *Random Number Table*.

If you posess Kai-surge, add 4 to this number. If you possess Kai-screen, add 2. If you possess Assimilance, add 1.

Also, if your current ENDURANCE points total is 18 or more, add 1; if your current ENDURANCE points total is 17 or less, deduct 1.

If your total score is now *3* or less, turn to **206**.
If it is *4–8*, turn to **305**.
If it is *9* or more, turn to **138**.

## 264

You are awoken in the middle of the night by an excruciating, vice-like pain that engulfs your whole head. With great difficulty you sit up and open your eyes and, at first, you assume that a new day must already have dawned for the cave is awash with a vivid white light. Then the pain in your head begins to ease and when you look out over the surrounding landscape, you see that the light has a far more sinister origin.

The sky is alive with hordes of glowing, wraith-like phantoms. They swoop down from the roiling storm clouds and skim the treetops, howling and screeching like insane banshees. A trio of these ghastly apparitions are hovering just a few metres from the cave mouth, from where they are assaulting you with a psychic bombardment. You muster your Magnakai skills to erect a psi-screen to protect your mind from their psychic attack, but your reflexes are pain-dulled and you lose 6 ENDURANCE points before your defence knits together.

Turn to **326**.

### 265

Weakened by the effects of the cursed water, you stagger away from the trough and very nearly drop your torch. Nearby, at the wayside altar, stands an acolyte Elder who is watching the procession. He notices your reaction after having dipped your hand into the trough and it makes him suspicious. He steps forwards and grabs your shoulder, commanding you to halt. Then you feel a tingling sensation, as if a horde of spiders were crawling in a line from your shoulder to the nape of your neck: the Elder has psychic abilities and he is attempting to probe your mind.

If you posses Kai-screen, turn to **78**.

If you do not possess this Grand Master Discipline, turn to **331**.

### 266

You crash down to earth amidst a heap of jagged stones and broken glass (lose 4 ENDURANCE points), but your quick wits and Kai senses help you roll away in time to avoid being hit by the deluge of burning timber that has been thrown up by the blast.

Adjust your ENDURANCE score and turn to **200**.

## 267

You focus your psychic energy at the distant druid and release a burst of power the instant he takes his eyes off you. You see him falter and place a hand to his forehead, as if he has just been struck by a stone.

Your sudden and unexpected use of a psychic attack caught the Arch Druid offguard. His inner mind is well shielded, but you sense that your burst of power has weakened him. Seizing this opportunity, you draw your weapon and rush forwards to attack him before he fully recovers.

Arch Druid Cadak:
COMBAT SKILL 45    ENDURANCE 32

If you win this combat, turn to **298**.

## 268

After a few minutes, the brigands suspect that one of their bolts has found its mark and they come creeping forwards. You inch your way back towards the copse, but before you can reach it you are intercepted by six brigands who come rushing across the rocks brandishing swords and daggers in their battle-scarred hands. You spring to your feet and unsheathe your weapon as they rush at you, stabbing and hacking with their gleaming blades.

Vakovarian brigands:
COMBAT SKILL 38    ENDURANCE 38

You may evade combat after six rounds, by turning to **59**.

If you win the fight, turn to **348**.

## 269

Using the Brotherhood spell of 'Mind Charm' you try to convince the Elder that you are what you outwardly appear to be — a lowly acolyte of Vashna. A wave of calm washes over him. He ceases to panic and his eyes flicker as if he is about to fall asleep, but you sense that he is fighting hard to resist your spell.

Pick a number from the *Random Number Table*.

For every level of Kai rank you have attained above the rank of Kai Grand Guardian, add 1 to the number you have picked.

If your total score is now 5 or less, turn to **177**.
If it is 6 or more, turn to **129**.

## 270

The screaming winds of the abyss rip and tear at you unmercifully as you are sucked through the heart of this whirling black vortex. All the while you cling to the Deathstaff, although its chill touch is far colder than even the frigid gales of the void and it drains you of warmth like some evil vampire (lose 5 ENDURANCE points).

Turn to **345**.

## 271

Unfortunately, you do not move swiftly enough to avoid the bolt. It gashes the side of your neck and opens a deep wound: lose 10 ENDURANCE points.

The shock of impact knocks you out of the saddle and you land amongst a tangle of roots and briars. Bracer continues on through the undergrowth and quickly disappears into a dense copse of pine trees. Gritting your teeth against the pain, you drag yourself free from the thorny foliage and crawl for cover among some moss-covered boulders nearby.

If you possess the Grand Master Discipline of Deliverance, turn to **253**.

If you do not, turn to **39**.

## 272

The hardened steel tip of your arrow penetrates the roof of the creature's mouth and skewers its brain. For a moment it freezes in mid-stride, seeming to defy gravity as it balances precariously on one hairy foot. Then its eyes roll back, revealing the whites, and it crashes down in an untidy heap at the side of the trail.

You bring your horse about and gallop away in case there are others of its kind lurking nearby. Beyond the plateau, the trail descends steeply towards a thick pine wood. Milky-white pools of water punctuate this section of the track, some deceptively deep, making the descent difficult and tiring. By the time you reach the wood your horse is in need of rest.

You dismount to take the weight off his back, and as

you gather his reins together you notice that the flap of your Backpack is undone. On checking the contents you discover that one of your possessions is missing. (Erase the second item on your list of Backpack Items. If you have only one item on your list, erase that one instead.)

As soon as your horse is rested, you remount him and set off through the pine wood, heading east.

Turn to **300**.


### 273

You unsheathe the twisted spike of black steel and thrust it into the swirling coils of energy that are holding you prisoner. There is a terrific *Crack!* as the tip penetrates the energy wall and, with a breathtaking suddenness, the wall disappears. You look down at the dagger in your hand but, to your astonishment, it too has disappeared (erase the Dagger of Vashna from your Special Items list).

To continue, turn to **132**.


### 274

You dash along the street, your eyes fixed on the shadowy archer as he makes his escape across the rooftops of the north quarter. You are twenty metres ahead of him when the street makes a turn and you find yourself faced by a solid brick wall; you have come to a dead end. You are about to retrace your steps when suddenly you notice a rusty iron staircase away to your right. It is a crude fire-escape ladder and it leads all the way to the roof of a linen warehouse. Quickly you climb the ladder, your weapon drawn in readiness to intercept the assassin the moment he appears.

Turn to **95**.

**275**

As soon as all of the acolytes have clambered aboard, you see them cut the grappling lines which tie their longboat to the sinking Vakovarian ship. At the longboat's prow there stand a trio of acolyte Elders, each holding a glowing wand of power in their outstretched hands. The moment they touch them together to form a triangle there is a flash of light. A swirling cone of vapour pours from the tip of this triangle and coils into the sky, creating a howling wind which fills the ship's sails and catapults the vessel away from the quayside at tremendous speed. Five minutes later the longboat has disappeared from sight, beyond the stormy horizon.

The raiding acolytes leave chaos behind them. The brigands flee in all directions, taking with them little more than the bitter regret that their hoard of loot is now resting in the hold of a sunken ship, ten fathoms down at the bottom of the quay. You leave Vorn as soon as you can and return to the copse to retrieve your horse. Then you set off on a trail that heads east, following along the shoreline of Lake Vorndarol. You pass a few brigands on this trail but they are too busy nursing their battle wounds to cause you any concern.

Three kilometres later, you come to a cove where the trail splits in two. The left trail continues on along the shoreline whilst the right trail turns towards the foothills of the Durncrags. Your natural tracking instincts tell you that the shoreline will be the harder of the two routes to follow. The hill trail looks easier, but it could take you much longer to reach the east shore of Lake Vorndarol that way.

If you wish to follow the shoreline trail, turn to **230**.

If you decide to take the foothills route, turn to **61**.

## 276

You draw on all your Kai mastery to evade these swooping horrors as you make good your escape. At first they pursue you, but when you leave the island they seem to lose interest and they turn back to their lair. Within a few minutes of their departing, a grey vapour boils up from the cracks in the ground. The vapour thickens with breathtaking speed until the basalt island and the entire fiery plain beyond is engulfed by this grey fog.

You walk through this cloying sea of mist for what seems like an eternity until your senses detect that something is circling high above you. At first you suspect that the golden-winged creatures have come hunting for you again, but then you detect that it is something completely different. There is only one creature, and you sense that it is using a highly-developed psychic probe in order to seek you out.

If you possess Grand Nexus, and have reached the Kai rank of Sun Knight, or higher, turn to **31**.

If you do not possess this skill, or if you have yet to attain this level of Kai mastery, turn to **106**.

## 277

Tearful with gratitude, the boy's parents kiss your hands and thank you with all their hearts for saving their child's life. The man asks if there is anything they can do to help you in return and you respond by asking who they are, and how they came to be hiding here.

You learn that they once lived in the hamlet of Vorn where the man, whose name is Bayan, made a humble-but-honest living fishing the waters of Lake Vorndarol. Then one fateful night, some weeks ago, the acolytes of Vashna came and destroyed Vorn. They managed to escape with their lives but they fear that the rest of their community were slaughtered in the attack, or perished in the dreadful storms which followed. For the past few weeks they have been hiding in the hills to avoid the acolytes and the marauding bands of robbers who have come from Vakovar looking for loot.

You tell them that you have been sent here by President Kadharian to find out what is going on at Lake Vorndarol. Bayan replies that he knows a safe route through the hills which leads directly to the ruins of his old home. He says he is willing to act as your guide and you accept his offer gratefully.

Turn to **335**.

## 278

'Fools!' screams Cadak at his fleeing acolytes. 'Must I do everything myself?'

With these words he bangs the tip of his staff three times against the floor of the dais and a gout of crackling energy arcs through the rain-laden air towards you. Instinctively, you raise the Deathstaff and catch the arching bolt on its haft. There is a flash of sparks, then the crackling energy flickers and disappears.

Cadak curses loudly and promises that you are about to die, but for all his bravado you sense that he is scared. He recognizes the Deathstaff for what it is and he fears that, in your hands, it could lay waste to all his meticulous plans. The aged druid looks to the stormy clouds and screams a command to the circling Vortexi to help him finish you once and for all.

Turn to **162**.

## 279

The first light of dawn brings with it a dramatic change in the weather. The storm has ended and the sky is now bright and clear, but on the distant horizon you can still see flashes of lightning and hear thunder rumbling in the mountains.

You leave the old mine and urge Bracer down the muddy slope towards the track, most of which you discover has been washed away by last night's storm. The damp earth is streaming in the unusual heat of the morning sun and the air crackles with an eerie residue of static electricity.

You continue your ride through the hills without stopping until, shortly after midday, you come to a derelict hovel which stands at the edge of a marshy peat bog. Your Kai senses inform you that there is somebody inside and, spurred on by curiosity, you resolve to find out who they are. You dismount and leave Bracer to feed on the marsh grass while you go forward to investigate the hovel on foot. You are six metres away from its rotting wooden door when suddenly it creaks open and you see an old man standing in the doorway. He is smiling at you.

If you have ever visited the city of Varetta, the city of Tahou, or a hut on the Ruanon Pike in a previous Lone Wolf adventure, turn to **220**.
If you have never visited any of these places, turn to **53**.

### 280

The man makes a slow, sure-footed descent to within three metres of where you are standing, during which time his weapon's sights never leave your chest. You can tell immediately that he is a skilled hunter and, judging by his furs and his beautifully crafted crossbow, he is a successful one too.

Your muscles are tense and coiled like springs, ready to propel you out of the path of his crossbow bolt in case he fires. But then he says something which makes you realize that, maybe, he has no intentions of killing you after all.

'You're no bandit,' he muses. 'No, by thunder, you look like a Sommlending to me.'

Turn to **340**.

### 281

A one-eyed mongrel is standing in front of the inn, its head cocked defiantly at the first-floor window through which you are observing the Vakovarians.

Mentally you command it to cease its infernal yapping and it responds by running away along the street, whimpering pathetically, as if it has just seen a ghost.

Most of the bandit activity appears to be going on around the quay. In order to get a better view, you leave the inn and make your way down through the ruins towards the lake, taking care to avoid those Vakovarians who are out looting. The burnt-out shell of a meeting hall offers you an unobstructed view of the quay and its flagstoned square. You hide here, invisible among the charred roof timbers, and watch as a curious scene unfolds on the quayside.

Turn to **163**.

## 282

The Demoness comes striding towards you, screaming maniacally, bolts of energy darting from her fingertips to rip open the ground as you zigzag to avoid being hit.

Pick a number from the *Random Number Table*.

If the number you have picked is *0–3*, turn to **4**. If it is *4–9*, turn to **92**.

## 283

The three phantoms swoop down into the trees as if to pursue the fleeing cats, but then they break off their attack and come speeding once more towards the mouth of the cave.

You sense a hostile psychic presence about them, an evil mind energy which is growing stronger as they draw nearer. You draw on your own formidable psychic skills and erect a defensive wall around your mind which keeps you safe from their first bombardment. Having encountered unexpected resistance, they veer upwards and vanish into the clouds. They have gone, but not for long. Within minutes they return with seven more of their ghostly brothers in train.

If you possess Kai-surge, and have reached the rank of Sun Lord, or higher, turn to **229**.

If you do not possess this Discipline, or if you have yet to attain this level of Kai rank, turn to **142**.

### 284

You level your weapon and strike out with deadly accuracy as the first of the vortexi engulf you.

Vortexi: COMBAT SKILL 49   ENDURANCE 38

For every level of Kai rank you have attained above that of Kai Grand Guardian, you may add a further 2 points to your COMBAT SKILL for the duration of this fight.

If you win the combat, turn to **46**.

### 285

In the cold light of dawn you see that the River Storn is too deep and fast-flowing to be fordable at this point. The trail follows the river downstream so you decide to follow it in the hope of finding somewhere to cross. Two kilometres later, you happen upon such a place.

At a point where the river slows and widens, you find

XVII.   A crossing can be achieved by boarding a raft and
pulling on its guide rope.

a crude rope ferry has been erected. It comprises two rafts attached to two long lengths of rope which are suspended above the river. A crossing can be achieved by boarding a raft and pulling on its guide rope to haul it across to the opposite bank.

You wait and observe that area for a few minutes. When you feel sure that it is safe to proceed, you place your horse aboard a raft and begin the laborious task of pulling yourself across to the distant shore.

Pick a number from the *Random Number Table*.

If the number you have picked is even (*0, 2, 4, 6, 8*), turn to **87**.
If it is odd (*1, 3, 5, 7, 9*), turn to **172**.

## 286

'Very well,' you say, 'how do you intend to help me?'

The young woman begins by confirming your suspicions. The Demoness Shamath is indeed preparing to go to the Maakengorge in response to Cadak's summons. She will make the journey by entering the tunnel; it is a shadow gate which will transport her from this plane of existence to Magnamund, to the great shimmering archway through which you were hurled by the storm. She will take with her an artefact of great evil – the Deathstaff – a device forged by the Dark God Naar himself and imbued with the power to resurrect the spirit of his long-lost champion, Lord Vashna, from the depths of the chasm of doom.

'Naar has laboured long and hard to create the Deathstaff,' says the young woman. She points once more towards the crystal dais and says, 'Can you see, Lone Wolf? It is there, resting beside Shamath's feet.'

Turn to **63**.

## 287

The drunkard gives a lop-sided grin and wipes his greasy mouth with the back of his hand before replying to your question.

'F' sure I know where be the Crooked Sage. Fine ale to be had there, if only I was moneyed enough to afford it. I'll tell you where it is for a small payment . . . say, ten gold crowns?

> If you wish to pay the drunkard for this information, erase 10 Gold Crowns from your *Action Chart* and turn to **62**.
>
> If you refuse to pay such a high price, turn to **185**.

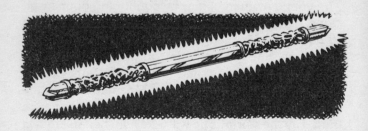

## 288

Coolly you stare into the eyes of the advancing acolytes as you summon forth the power-word of the Elder-magi: *Gloar*.

The sound hits them like a massive, invisible

hammer. It crushes their ribs and leaves their bodies lying broken and lifeless amongst the charred debris.

Turn to **325**.

### 289

Your search uncovers the following items:

Enough food for 3 Meals
Quiver
4 Arrows
Bow
3 Daggers
Tinderbox
Rope
Bottle of Wine

If you wish to keep any of the above, remember to make the appropriate adjustments to your *Action Chart*.

To leave the hut, turn to **143**.

### 290

You watch helplessly as the woman approaches, her corpse-white hands outstretched, reaching in eager anticipation for the flap of the money pouch which hangs from your belt. You fight to resist the mind charm which is paralysing your limbs but, try as you will, you cannot break free.

Then with a jolt, the feeling suddenly returns to your paralysed body. The woman has vanished and so, too, have nearly all the Gold Crowns in your belt pouch.

Pick a number from the *Random Number Table*.

**291**

If the number you have picked is *0–3*, there are only two Gold Crowns left in your pouch.

If the number you have picked is *4–7*, there are only three Gold Crowns remaining.

If the number you have picked is *8–9*, you have been left with five Gold Crowns.

Remember to adjust your *Action Chart* accordingly.

Cursing your luck, you coax your horse to the right at the road junction and continue on your search for the Crooked Sage Inn. A warren of covered alleyways and narrow passages eventually lead to a wider street, one which is illuminated by flickering torchlight.

Turn to **147**.

**291**

Like a fleeting shadow, you move through the undergrowth towards the brigand leader without making a sound. As you draw closer, you hear him cursing the incompetence of his men and you see him beating his clenched fist on the trunk of the fallen bough in frustration. Then you leap upon him, covering his mouth with one hand and locking his arm behind his back with the other. He growls and struggles like an angry bear to break free from your grip, but when you whisper a threat in his ear he quickly ceases to resist. Suddenly his nerve seems to break and he begins to whimper like a frightened puppy. You ease your hand away from his mouth just enough to allow him to speak and at once he pleads with you not to kill him. He offers you the

contents of his satchel and free passage away from
here if you will promise not to harm him.

If you wish to see what he has in his satchel, turn
to **113**.

If you wish to question him about why he has laid
an ambush for you, turn to **75**.

### 292

The Elder becomes angry. He scolds you for more
than a minute before he loses his patience and stalks
off, dismissing you as unworthy of his time. Those
seated around you have now become uncomfortably curious about who you are. To avoid their
attentions, you get up and move to the stern where
a score of acolytes are kneeling in prayer.

Turn to **124**.

### 293

The yellow blossoms are surprisingly nutritious:
restore 3 ENDURANCE points. If you wish, you can
gather some more of these blooms as you continue
your ride across the plateau, and store them in your
backpack (up to a maximum of 2 Meals).

Turn to **18**.

### 294

You whisper the words of the Brotherhood spell
'Mind Charm' and, at once, you see Smudd relaxing
under its influence. He removes his hand from his
sword and the scowl of fearful suspicion softens to a
smile as he lowers himself back into his seat. With a
flick of his hand he dismisses the bar-girl. She leaves

without protest and as you watch her walk away, he leans across the table and says, 'How can I help you, stranger?'

'What do you know about a little hamlet called Vorn?' you say, quietly.

For a moment the look of suspicion returns to his beady eyes, then he sneers and says, 'I know it no longer exists, that's what I know. There's rumour on the street that it was destroyed by the storms, but there's more to it than that. More than I care to remember.'

You show him the Black Amulet that President Kadharian gave to you and once more you repeat your question. Now he refuses to answer, fearing that you are one of Kadharian's agents out to arrest him. He kicks back his chair and tries to stand, but he does not make it.

He is halfway out of his seat when suddenly his chest is transfixed by a crystal arrow. Wide-eyed with pain and shocked surprise, he crashes to the floor amid a spray of blood and spilt ale.

Turn to **215**.

## 295

You take your place among the throng who are kneeling before the dais, and watch as the tall, platinum-haired figure begins to speak.

'I, Cadak of Kaag, summon forth from the Vortex of the Planes the Deliverer of Vashna, Mighty Lord of Darkness, Prince of the Legions of the Restless Dead,' he says, his words clear and confident above the howling storm. 'Come to us. Come to us now and fulfil our destiny. We, the worthy, now prove our faith in the undying power of Vashna.'

Upon hearing these words, the acolytes utter a chilling cry of affirmation and rise to their feet. By rank they follow the Elders in single file towards a smaller, shimmering metallic arch which stands to one side of the crystal dais, almost obscured by the glare of the larger one. One by one they file through this archway, under the watchful gaze of Cadak, and then return to their places where they kneel and pray.

As you approach the smaller arch, you sense a curtain of power drawn across it. Anxiously you pray to the Gods Kai and Ishir to protect you as you prepare to pass through this invisible barrier.

If you possess the Sommerswerd, turn to **166**.

If you do not possess this Special Item, turn to **204**.

## 296

The night passes uneventfully, but you awake at dawn to a spectacular sight. The eastern sky is filled with soaring meteors of fiery yellow light which shoot from the midst of a bank of deep magenta storm clouds. The air seethes with electrical energy and lightning flashes can be seen all along the distant horizon. You find the sight unnerving, doubly so when you calculate that its centre of activity lies directly over the Maakengorge.

After a frugal breakfast, you set off along the shoreline trail on a route which takes you ever-nearer to the storm.

Pick a number from the *Random Number Table*.

If the number you have picked is *0–4*, turn to **32**. If it is *5–9*, turn to **155**.

## 297

You thank Gwynian for his help and he waves farewell as you leave the hovel and walk back to your horse.

'Good luck, Grand Master,' he calls out, 'my hopes and my prayers go with you.'

By nightfall you have covered twenty kilometres of rough terrain and have been assailed by extremes of weather. From a desert-like heat at mid-afternoon the temperature plummeted, causing a sub-zero squall which left you and Bracer blanketed with frost. But now, as darkness draws its cloak over this troubled land, the temperature quickly rises. This heralds the return of the rain, and the thunder and the violent lightning strikes.

Helped by your tracking skills, you discover a shallow cave where you can take shelter from the storm. You are tired and hungry, and unless you possess Grand Huntmastery, you must now eat a Meal or lose 3 ENDURANCE points.

If you possess Animal Mastery, and have attained the rank of Kai Grand Guardian, or higher, turn to **194**.

If you do not possess this Discipline, or if you have yet to achieve this level of Kai mastery, turn to **23**.

## 298

As you strike your killing blow, Cadak shudders and crashes to the ground, clutching his staff tightly to his chest. He finds just enough strength to utter a dying curse, then, before your disbelieving eyes, his body slowly disintegrates. The skin is quickly criss-crossed by thousands of wrinkles, and the drying flesh falls from his skull, leaving it bare boned with a tattered layer of leathery skin stretched over it. Then, in the next instant his body collapses into naked bone. His staff breaks into chalky chunks and, finally, bone and staff blacken and fall away to dust.

Turn to **72**.

## 299

You crash down to earth amidst a heap of jagged stones and broken glass. Then, as you are struggling to stand, a deluge of burning timber falls on your back and knocks you down: lose 9 ENDURANCE points.

If you are still alive, turn to **200**.

## 300

It is dusk when you emerge from the woods and ride along a ridge which overlooks the eastern shoreline of Lake Vorndarol, and it is here that you catch your first glimpse of the acolyte settlement. It consists of several long huts, grouped around a great hall of stone on a hill overlooking a shingle beach. Down on the beach there is a wooden jetty where an acolyte longboat is moored. It is the same longboat that was used in the attack on Vorn quay.

Cautiously, you descend the ridge and ride towards the settlement. When you are within half a kilometre of the perimeter, you leave your horse and go forwards on foot. There are acolytes everywhere but you find it easy to avoid them and enter the encampment unseen. Under cover of the approaching darkness and aided by your camouflage skills, you make your way towards the stone hall. You sense that something important is going on there and you resolve to find out what it is.

Turn to **137**.

**301**

Swiftly you unshoulder your bow, draw an arrow from your quiver, and take hurried aim as the man in black leaps from the window ledge on to the balcony.

Pick a number from the *Random Number Table*. If you possess the Discipline of Grand Weaponmastery with Bow, add 3 to the number you have picked.

If your total score is now 6 or less, turn to **27**.
If it is 7 or more, turn to **251**.

### 302

Your mastery of the Kai pathsmanship Discipline warns you that you could be ambushed if you were to enter the circle of boulders. Forewarned, you wait and observe the horseshoe of rocks a while longer. Before too long your patience is rewarded: something is moving around down there.

You intensify your vision and see that it is a pack of bony, dog-like creatures. They are feeding on something in the lee of the rocks.

If you wish to go and see what it is they are feeding upon, turn to **11**.

If you choose to avoid the horseshoe rocks, turn to **248**.

### 303

Aching with fatigue and spattered with the foul ichor that passed for blood in the bodies of Shamath's attendants, you step back from those you have slain and stare defiantly at the towering Demoness.

Turn to **242**.

### 304

You draw back your arrow until the feathers are touching your lips, then you let slip the straining bowstring. The shaft whistles through the trees towards the brigand leader's back and hits him squarely between the shoulder blades with a loud *Thok!* He screams, and throws his arms wide as he crashes face-first to the ground.

His henchmen spin around and see you. They bellow commands to their underlings and at once the angry brigands begin to close in on your position from all sides. You retreat into the trees and head back the way you came, anxious to retrieve your horse before the brigands find him. You are within a stone's throw of Bracer when suddenly you are confronted by more than a dozen bandits, hungry for revenge. They attack in a frenzy and you are forced to fight all twelve at once.

Vakovarian brigands:
COMBAT SKILL 46    ENDURANCE 56

You may evade this combat after six rounds by turning to **35**.

If you win the fight, turn to **188**.

### 305

You wield the Deathstaff with confidence, but the insidious effect of the weapon is making you careless as you sweep the staff around your head. Some of the stronger vortexi are able to break away from the spinning cyclone to make good their attack.

Vortexi: COMBAT SKILL 40    ENDURANCE 30

For every level of Kai rank you have attained above that of Kai Grand Guardian, you may add 2 to your COMBAT SKILL for the duration of this fight. However, due to the harmful side effects of the Deathstaff, you must reduce your ENDURANCE score by 2 prior to the start of this combat.

If you win the combat, turn to **46**.

### 306

The creature roars with frustration. Mentally its instincts are pulling it apart; it cannot decide whether to attack or retreat. Finally, with a howl of anger, it comes lumbering towards you. It is going to attack but you sense that your commands have greatly weakened its resolve.

You raise your weapon and bring your horse about to face the beast, but on the instant he sees the creature he panics and rears up on his hind legs, neighing with fright. You bring him under control using your innate Kai skills, but in doing so your attention is diverted from the attacking beast as it moves in and swipes at you with its clawed paw.

Black corvayl: COMBAT SKILL 38    ENDURANCE 56

Reduce your COMBAT SKILL by 5 for the first round of this fight only.

If you win the combat, turn to **210**.

### 307

Your Magnakai pathsmanship skills and the freshness of the mud make it easy for you to tell that the tracks are made by humans on foot. You count at least six different sets of footprints, all heading in a north-easterly direction.

Turn to **67**.

### 308

Your weapon disintegrated in the blast (erase it from your *Action Chart*), yet it served to conduct the energy of the lightning ball away from your body. It has spared you from sustaining injury and possibly death.

Dazed by the blast and the fall, you stagger to your

feet and look around for your horse. He has halted at the river's edge where he is pacing nervously to and fro. You call to him, using your natural Kai skills to calm and control his fear, and he responds at once and returns to collect you. Swiftly you climb back into the saddle and gallop away along the river trail, anxious to put distance between you and this deadly storm.

Turn to **80**.

## 309

You leap into the saddle and steer your horse away from the lake and the sinister circle of boulders. Then you hear another frenzied howl and you glance over your shoulder to see a pack of eight ridge-backed jackals come streaming through a gap in the boulders, drawn by the scent of your horse. They seem to know that he is in a weakened state and this fuels their fury.

You urge your horse to the gallop as the jackals bound along the shore, but he is weakening fast and the ground here is treacherous: it is strewn with loose rocks and jagged shale.

If you possess Grand Huntmastery, and have reached the rank of Kai Grand Guardian or higher, turn to **112**.

If you do not possess this Discipline, or have yet to attain this level of Kai rank, turn to **99**.

## 310

You make it across the street to the roof, but you twist your ankle on landing and crash heavily against the corrugated tiles: lose 2 ENDURANCE points.

Painfully you limp to your feet and watch as the assassin makes good his escape. For a moment he halts beside a tall chimney stack and turns to look in your direction. Then three other shadowy figures emerge from behind the stack and stand at his shoulder. They stare at you silently for a few moments before turning and melting away into the night.

Having decided it would be pointless to try to follow them, you make your way down from the roof and retrace your steps back to the stables of the Crooked Sage in order to collect your horse.

Turn to **341**.

## 311

Stunned by the speed and skill with which you have dispatched over fifteen of their brothers, the circle of murderous acolytes retreat a few paces to catch their breath and lick their wounds.

'We have an intruder in our midst,' screams Cadak, levelling his wizard's staff at you accusingly. The tip flares brightly, then a jet of crimson energy comes arching towards your chest. You try to dodge it but it follows you and connects with your spine, numbing your limbs with its insidious effect.

Turn to **228**.

## 312

The brigand captain's men respond to his call for help and, with the sound of them closing in, you break off the fight and take to your heels. Thinking that he has terrified you into running away, the captain gives chase, but he soon loses you among the dense pines and calls off his pursuit. The area is alive with bandits and you are forced to flee northwards, away from the place where you left Bracer tethered to a tree. You are anxious for his safety and mindful that there are still many miles to be covered before you reach Lake Vorndarol, but you dare not turn back for him. Then you hear something that makes you halt in your tracks: it is the sound of a horse whinnying.

Turn to **223**.

### 313

You fight to maintain your grip but you have been badly weakened during your conflict with Shamath and Cadak, and your reserves of strength are exhausted. Comforted by the knowledge that your actions have prevented the resurrection of Vashna and the destruction of your homeland, you finally release your grip and allow yourself to be sucked to your doom in the whirling abyss.

Heroically, your life and your quest end here.

### 314

For a moment the Elder is wide-eyed and speechless with shock, but you know that he will soon come to his senses and raise the alarm. You must act swiftly and decisively if you are to prevent him from revealing your true identity to the others on this boat.

If you possess Kai-alchemy, and wish to use it, turn to **269**.

If you possess Magi-magic, and wish to use it, turn to **107**.

If you possess neither of these Disciplines, or you do not wish to use them, turn to **37**.

**315**

Immediately you recognize the tall, muscular man who stands before you now; he was once known as the Slavemaster of Aarnak. He was an agent of the Elder Magi based in the Darklands who, seven years earlier, helped you to enter the dread city of Helgedad and bring about the downfall of the Darklords. Now he is known by a different name – President Kadharian of Magador.

'Welcome, Grand Master,' he says, smiling warmly, 'it seems we have both come a long way since our last meeting.'

The President is amused by your expression of surprise and offers an explanation of how he came to be leader of this rough republic. After the fall of Helgedad, the Elder Magi arranged for his safe passage to the Stornlands where he was granted a command in the army of Lyris. He distinguished himself in battle and later, once the remains of the Darkland armies had been vanquished, he returned to his native Magador and led an uprising against King Vanagrom VI, who had long been a puppet of the Darklords. The revolt ended with the king's death and the abolition of the monarchy. Magador became a republic and the Slavemaster, whose given name was Kadharian, became its first elected leader.

'And now to the reasons why I have requested your help, Grand Master,' he says, as he pushes open the door to a smaller room which adjoins the senate hall.

Turn to **100**.

## 316

You cast the glowing token into the darkness and it explodes with a dull boom among the boulders, showering the path with dirt and slivers of stone. (Erase this Special Item from your *Action Chart*.)

The sudden flash and bang cause a moment of panic among the acolytes. They fear that they are being attacked by Vakovarians and many of them drop their torches and run back along the path, screaming excitedly. Using this confusion to your advantage, you attempt to tag on to the end of the line of acolytes who are still advancing up the path.

Pick a number from the *Random Number Table*. If you possess Assimilance, add 3 to the number you have picked. If you possess Kai-screen, add 2.

If your total score is now 6 or less, turn to **245**. If it is 7 or more, turn to **41**.

## 317

The few scavengers that survive the attack wheel away and return to the mountains, cawing with frustration, their wings bloodied and their hunger unsatiated.

You manage to regain control of the raft and, at length, you reach the far side of the river and disembark safely. A stony trail runs along the bank, heading north, and you follow it with high hopes of reaching Lake Vorndarol before sunset. All day the sun blazes supreme in a cloudless sky and waves of heat create a shimmering, distorted view of the trail ahead. The distant horizon is streaked with myriad colours and the dry air crackles with electricity, a legacy of last night's violent storm. Late in the afternoon you come to the ruins of an ancient settlement and stop here to allow your horse to rest awhile in the shade.

If you possess Grand Pathsmanship, turn to **102**.
If you do not possess this Discipline, turn to **260**.

### 318

You step back from the glowing remains of Helshezag and feel yourself sagging beneath the unnatural weight of the Deathstaff. The sound of the bolt attracts Shamath's attention and she spins around to stare at you, sending her attendants flying in all directions. Then she screams with unholy anger and the noise of her wrath lifts you bodily and sends you skidding across the floor.

Desperately you fight to maintain your grip on the Deathstaff as the furious Demoness gets to her feet. She comes striding towards you, bolts of energy darting from her fingertips to rip open the ground as you stumble away towards the yawning black tunnel. The deafening shriek of her voice rings in your ears as you clutch the Deathstaff to your chest and leap head first into the oblivion of the shadow gate.

Turn to **270**.

### 319

The ground beneath Bracer's hooves is trembling. At first you think the thunder is the cause, but then you notice that the sound of the storm is getting louder and louder. Fear knots your stomach when suddenly you see a solid roaring wall of water come tumbling down the gulley. It is a flash flood and, unless you act quickly, you and your horse will be washed away without trace.

XVIII. You see a solid roaring wall of water come tumbling down the gulley.

If you possess Grand Huntmastery and have reached the Kai rank of Grand Guardian, or higher, turn to **104**.

If you do not possess this skill, or have yet to attain this rank of Kai Grand Mastership, turn to **73**.

## 320

You focus your sight and hearing at the bushes and suddenly realize that you have been taken in by an elaborate ruse. A thin length of twine runs away under the foliage; it is the trigger that dislodged the rock and made it fall. There is nobody hiding there after all.

Your eye follows the twine along the hillside to a boulder high up on the slope to your left. Perhaps your would-be ambusher is hiding there instead?

If you possess Grand Nexus, and have reached the Kai rank of Sun Knight, turn to **214**.

If you do not possess this skill, or have yet to reach this level of Kai mastery, turn to **146**.

## 321

A lightning ball is hurtling directly towards you. Desperately, you pull your horse away to avoid being hit but the fiery meteor changes course in mid-flight as if guided by an unseen hand. You make one last attempt to dodge it but to no avail; it impacts upon the hilt of the Sommerswerd and you are thrown from the saddle amidst a shower of glowing sparks.

Pick a number from the *Random Number Table* (0 = 10). The number you have picked is equal to the number of ENDURANCE points lost as a result of the lightning impact and the fall.

After making the necessary adjustments to your *Action Chart*, turn to **51**.

### 322

As you draw level with the first Elder he reaches down and takes hold of your shoulder to make you halt. He says something in a dialect you do not understand and, when you do not answer, his suspicion swiftly turns to anger. He grabs your robe and pulls it open, revealing your leather tunic and breeches. Recognizing them at once to be Sommlending in origin, he gasps with shock as he guesses at your true identity.

'Seize him!' bellows the other Elder, and a score of acolytes spring forward to obey the command. You draw your weapon and fight them with breathtaking skill and valour, but eventually you are overcome by the sheer weight of their numbers. By the time they have disarmed you and pinned you to the ground, more than thirty of them lie slain or seriously injured in a heaped circle around where you lie.

You stare back defiantly at the ring of grim torchlit faces that loom over you. Then the face of an acolyte Elder comes into view and he sneers with disdain. He places the tip of a glowing wand to your forehead and suddenly there is an explosion of white light. Sadly for you, it is the last sensation you will ever experience.

Your life and your quest end here.

### 323

Smudd is clearly impressed by your generosity. He removes his hand from his sword and the scowl of fearful suspicion softens to a smile as he lowers himself back into his seat. With a flick of his hand he dismisses the bar-girl. She leaves without protest, and as you watch her walk away, he leans across the table and says,

'How can I help you, stranger?'

'What do you know about a little hamlet called Vorn?' you say, quietly. For an instant the look of suspicion returns to his beady eyes, then he sneers and says,

'I know it no longer exists, that's what I know. There's a rumour on the street that it was destroyed by the storm, but there's more to it than that. More than I care to remember.'

You show him the Black Amulet that President Kadharian gave to you and once more you repeat your question. Now he refuses to answer, fearing that you are one of Kadharian's agents out to arrest him. He kicks back his chair and tries to stand, but he does not make it.

He is halfway out of his seat when suddenly his chest is transfixed by a crystal arrow. Wide-eyed with pain and shocked surprise, he crashes to the floor amid a spray of blood and spilt ale.

Turn to **215**.

## 324

The few acolytes who survive the fight count themselves lucky and flee for their lives.

'Fools!' screams Cadak, at his routing acolytes. 'Must I do everything myself!'

With these words he bangs the tip of his staff three times against the floor of the dais and a gout of crackling energy arcs through the rain-laden air towards you. Instinctively, you raise the Deathstaff and catch the arcing bolt on its haft. There is a flash of sparks, then the crackling energy flickers and disappears.

Cadak curses loudly and promises that you are about to die, but for all his bravado you sense that he is scared. He recognizes the Deathstaff for what it is and he fears that, in your hands, it could lay waste to all his meticulous plans. The aged druid looks to the stormy clouds and screams a command to the circling vortexi to help him finish you once and for all.

Turn to **65**.

## 325

Suddenly a piercing note blares out above the din of battle: it is a war-horn and it is sounding the recall to the acolyte longboat. You see those acolytes of Vashna who are fighting in the ruins suddenly break off their combat and race back to the quay in answer to this command. Their mission has been achieved. They have recaptured their three brothers and now the time has come for them to depart.

As you watch them streaming along the body-strewn quay, a bold plan springs to mind, a plan that could enable you quickly to discover the truth about what is happening at the Maakengorge. If you were to don a red robe from one of the acolytes you have slain, you could infiltrate the ranks of those acolytes who are now fleeing back to the longboat.

If you wish to put on a red robe and attempt to get aboard the acolyte longboat, turn to **76**.

If you decide that it is too dangerous a plan, you can watch the acolyte retreat from the safety of the ruins, by turning to **275**.

### 326

The trio of phantoms break off their attack and take to the sky to rejoin their unholy siblings. As their wispy, glowing forms disappear into the stormy clouds, you get to your feet and quickly gather up your weapons and equipment. They have gone, but not for long. Within minutes they return with seven more of their ghostly brothers in train.

If you possess Kai-screen, and have reached the rank of Kai Grand Guardian, or higher, turn to **111**.

If you do not possess this Discipline, or if you have yet to attain this level of Kai rank, turn to **30**.

### 327

Before you stretches a gigantic cavern. Its walls of ancient obsidian rise to a high-arched roof where hangs a circle of stalagtites — twelve huge luminescent spears of lime-green stone. Bathed in their pulsating glow is a many-tiered crystal dais, identical to the one on which Arch Druid Cadak stood before the great shimmering archway at the edge of the Maakengorge. To the right of this dais you see a dark tunnel. The entrance appears like a black semi-circular shadow upon the cavern wall.

Standing upon the uppermost tier of the dais is a creature which both mesmerizes and repulses you. It has the semblance of a human female, yet she stands more than seven metres tall. She is strikingly beautiful but you sense at once that she is also wholly evil. Her skin has a deathly, corpse-like pallor and she is clad in a flowing black costume which trails thin wisps of smoke. Cloaked figures scurry around the lower tiers of the dais, carrying out their mistress's commands and attending to her every whim. If they fail or displease her she crushes them like lowly insects in her elegant, deadly hands.

You watch in silent fascination as this demonic creature makes preparations, as if for a long journey. Then, in a flash of a sudden realization, you know her purpose. She is getting ready to enter the tunnel, a tunnel which will transport her to the archway at the edge of the Maakengorge. She is the deliverer of Vashna of whom Cadak spoke, the one who will raise the spirit of Lord Vashna from the chasm of doom!

Suddenly you are aware that someone is standing behind you. Instantly, you unsheathe your weapon and spin around to face them, half-expecting to see the grotesque face of a demonic minion. Instead, you find yourself looking into the impish face of a young teenage girl.

Turn to **173**.

You let loose your arrow and watch as it clips the man's thigh before arcing away into the night. You hear him yelp with pain, but the wound is superficial and it does not prevent him from making a safe landing on the rooftop opposite.

You dash along the street, your eyes fixed on the

XIX.  You find yourself looking into the impish face of a
young teenage girl.

limping archer as he makes good his escape from the inn. You are twenty metres ahead of him when the street makes a turn and you find yourself face-to-face with a solid brick wall; you have come to a dead end. You are about to retrace your steps when suddenly you notice a rusty iron staircase away to your right. It is a crude fire-escape ladder and it leads all the way to the roof of a linen warehouse. Quickly you climb the ladder, your weapon drawn in readiness to intercept the wounded assassin the moment he appears.

Turn to **95**.

The Vakovarians search the inn thoroughly. They fail to find you on their first sweep, but when they return to search again, one of them discovers your hiding place when he accidentally treads on your foot.

You react quickly and with fatal effect. A blow to the throat silences the brigand for good and prevents him from ever warning his confederates that you are here. They do not notice that he is missing and they leave the inn to go elsewhere. By the time they realize they are one man short, you have searched and hidden his body and made good your escape from the inn.

Among the items you discover on the brigand are the following:

Bow
Quiver with 4 arrows
Dagger
Short Sword

13 Gold Crowns
Rope
Small Sack

After leaving the inn, you make your way down through the ruins towards the lake, taking care to avoid other Vakovarians who are out looting. The burnt-out shell of a meeting hall offers you an unobstructed view of the quay and its flagstoned square. You hide here, invisible among the charred roof timbers, and watch as a curious scene unfolds on the quayside.

Turn to **163**.

## 330

The brigands are clumsy in their eagerness to reach the copse, presenting themselves as easy targets to your bow. Every arrow finds its mark until their leader calls off the assault and they take cover among the boulders. Now the trees echo to the sound of steel bolts ripping through branches and ricocheting off stone; once more these brigands have begun firing at you with their crossbows.

Pick a number from the *Random Number Table* $(0 = 10)$. The number you have picked is equal to the number of arrows you have fired at the brigands (adjust your *Action Chart* accordingly).

If the number you have picked is greater than the number of arrows you have in your quiver, erase them all and turn to **268**.

If, after having deducted the relevant number of arrows, you still have one or more left in your quiver, turn to **167**.

### 331

You draw on your Magnakai Discipline of Psi-screen to keep safe your identity from the Elder's mind probe. You sense that his psychic power is strong and you fear that your defences may not be sufficient to repel him.

Pick a number from the *Random Number Table*. If you possess Assimilance, add 3 to the number you have picked. Also, if you possess Grand Nexus, add 2; and if you possess Kai-alchemy, add 1.

If your total score is now *8* or less, turn to **160**. If it is *9* or more, turn to **181**.

### 332

You ride slowly through the clammy fog which carpets the cobblestones of this ill-smelling lane. Clamped against the walls of the surrounding buildings are oil-soaked torches which serve to illuminate the signs of wine shops and taverns. They are crudely painted with emblems — a bloodied battle-axe, a winged horse, a watery sun rising from a broken skull. There is not one that resembles a crooked sage and you are beginning to lose heart when suddenly you hear the sound of drunken revelry coming from a two-storey building at the end of the street. Its oaken doors hang open and the vivid orange glare of its roaring hearth spills invitingly into the dank night gloom. Although it has no painted emblem, you sense at once that you have at last found the Crooked Sage Inn.

At your approach, a sallow-faced stable boy limps from a wooden hut which is leaning precariously against the side of the tavern wall. For one Gold

Crown (erase this from your *Action Chart*), he takes charge of your horse and shows you to the taproom door.

Turn to **21**.

### 333

Your punch lifts the Elder clean off his feet and sends him tumbling over the side of the boat. A cry goes up along the deck, a shout of alarm that one of the Elders has fallen overboard. Scores of acolytes rush to the rail in response but there is nothing they can do. The longboat is travelling so fast that he is already hundreds of metres behind the stern and cannot be seen amidst the churning water.

Fortunately, none of the acolytes saw you throw your punch; they all assume the Elder fell accidentally. However, those who were seated near you have now become uncomfortably curious about who you are. To avoid their attentions, you move to the stern where you find a score of acolytes kneeling in prayer.

Turn to **124**.

### 334

You rush towards the crystal dais, feinting and weaving to avoid the oncoming automatons. But the machine-like warriors move closer together and, by the time you reach them, they have closed ranks and you run straight into their solid wall. You will have to fight them. These beings are immune to all forms of psychic attack (except *Kai Blast*).

Shamath automatons:
COMBAT SKILL 38    ENDURANCE 60

You may evade combat after four rounds by turning to **153**.

If you win this fight, turn to **240**.

### 335

Bayan says farewell to his wife, warning her to stay hidden here with the child until he returns. She thanks you once more for curing her son and she wishes you a safe journey, then Bayan leads you to another hovel where he has hidden a donkey. It is a stubborn, flea-bitten old ass, but it serves Bayan well as the two of you follow his secret trail into the foothills of the southern Durncrags.

It is a long and tortuous route but it is also a safe one. At dusk you come to a cave whose entrance is hidden by clumps of loose brushwood. Bayan and his family have used it several times over in the past few weeks and they have stocked it with a buried cache of roots and berries. These, together with some live game which you catch at a nearby stream, make for a filling and nutritious meal which you both enjoy before settling down to a long sleep.

You may restore your ENDURANCE points score to its original level. To continue, turn to **64**.

### 336

The creature roars with anger as it overcomes your mental commands and rushes forward. You raise your weapon and bring your horse about to face this fearsome beast's attack. The instant he sees the creature he panics and rears up on his hind legs, neighing with fright, his hooves scrabbling frantically at the air. You bring him under control using your innate Kai skills, but in so doing your attention is diverted from the attacking beast as it moves in and swipes at you with its clawed paw.

Black corvayl: COMBAT SKILL 46    ENDURANCE 58

Reduce your COMBAT SKILL by 10 for the first round of this fight only.

If you win the combat, turn to **210**.

### 337

You leave the cave at first light and continue your lonely trek towards Lake Vorndarol. Before dawn, an icy wind swept down from the north and spread a thick blanket of frost on the trail, freezing the mud beneath. To your surprise, the going is easier and swifter than expected and, by noon, you find you have covered more than thirty kilometres.

During your ride you have watched the land slowly changing. The trail is now steeper and granite outcroppings have begun to appear, tinged with moss and interspersed with pine trees and grey-green underbrush. You are approaching an area littered with huge granite boulders when suddenly your Magnakai pathsmanship skills alert you to danger; you sense there is an ambush ahead.

Pick a number from the *Random Number Table*.

If the number you have picked is *0–1*, turn to **182**.
If it is *2–9*, turn to **241**.

### 338

While you enjoy your impromptu meal, you stare at the shimmering waters of the lake, now some ten kilometres distant, and contemplate with dread what may await you when you get to the east shore. Then, unexpectedly, your sixth sense warns you that danger is much closer at hand and instinctively you reach for your weapon. As your hand closes upon it, a fearful roar erupts from the bushes on the other side of the trail. Suddenly the foliage is torn open by two great hairy paws and a black, bear-like hulk comes charging across the trail towards you, its fanged jaw open as if to bite.

If you possess Animal Mastery, and wish to use it, turn to **15**.

If you have a Bow and wish to use it, turn to **198**.

If you have neither, or choose not to use them, turn to **257**.

## 339

Although you are unable to sleep, you take some comfort from the fact that there is no storm this night. You leave the grove at first light and follow the rushing stream until you happen upon a shallow bend where the water is fordable on horseback. You cross here, make a wide detour, and then return to the trail a mile beyond the Vakovarian's encampment.

The trail gradually descends towards the burnt and derelict hovels of Vorn, clustered in squalid disarray around a greystone quay. Vakovarian bandits occupy the ruined hamlet and you decide it wise to leave the trail in case they have posted a lookout. A copse of stunted firs offers you a good hiding place for your horse. You tether him here, then gather some grasses and roots for him to eat while you are away scouting the hamlet.

You have no difficulty entering Vorn unseen. From the first-floor ruins of a burnt-out inn on the outskirts of the hamlet you make a careful observation of the Vakovarians. They seem to be systematically looting the ruins and transporting their ill-gotten booty to a fishing boat which is moored at the quay. You are watching this boat closely when suddenly your concentration is broken by the sound of a yapping dog.

If you possess Animal Mastery, turn to **281**.
If you do not possess this Discipline, turn to **2**.


**340**

'I bid you welcome, Northlander,' says the fur-clad stanger, taking you aback with his friendly tone, 'T'as been many moons since I've seen a welcome face in this godforsaken land. What beckons you here?'

You answer with caution in case he is trying to trick you, and simply reply that you are a hunter.

'A hunter, eh?' he says, smiling. 'Come, now. You be no hunter, least none like I know. And I should know seein' as I'm a hunter m'self.'

You use your Kai senses to assess this man's purpose and realize that he is speaking the truth. He really is a hunter and he intends you no harm.

'Very well,' you say, 'I admit I'm not a hunter, at least not in the way you think. I've come here to find out what is going on at the Maakengorge. I want to know why Vorn was destroyed and what is causing the storms. But what of your purpose, master hunter? What quarry is there here that's worth battling these accursed storms for?'

## 341

The hunter tells you that he has travelled all the way from Karkaste, in the realm of Lyris, to hunt for black corvayl. The fur of this beast is worth a small fortune in the markets of Casiorn and the Stornlands. He says the storms and the Vakovarian brigands have made things difficult for him; he has been in these mountains for more than a month now and has only two pelts to show for his trouble.

The hunter, whose name is Fyrad, invites you to join him at his camp in the hills. It will soon be dusk and the icy winds are getting colder, so you gladly accept his offer of food and warm shelter.

Turn to **175**.

## 341

As soon as the stable boy has saddled Bracer, you mount up and leave the inn at a gallop. You decide to forgo sleep this night and begin your journey north without further delay. Shortly past midnight, you pass through Helgor's ruined East Gate and head off along a rutted track that winds a north-easterly route towards the River Storn. The moon is full and this rough trail is illuminated clearly by its cold, ashen light. Far to the north an electrical storm is brewing. Flashes of forked lightning light up the horizon and the sky, and the hills echo to the rumble of distant thunder.

You have covered little more than ten kilometres when the trail gradually peters out. You continue on across soft heathland for a few miles further until you find another trail, muddier than the first. Fresh tracks are imprinted in its surface, leading off towards the north-east. Curious as to their origin, you dismount and take a closer look.

Pick a number from the *Random Number Table*. If you have Grand Huntmastery, add 1 for every Kai level you are above the rank of Kai Grand Guardian to the number you have picked.

If your total score is now 4 or less, turn to **307**.
If it is 5 or more, turn to **256**.

### 342

The horse refuses to approach the trees so you dismount and tether him to a boulder before investigating the wooded gulley on foot. Beyond the perimeter of trees you discover a clearing where a score of shallow graves are clustered in a circle. You scrape away some of the stones and earth from the nearest grave and uncover the corpse of a man clad in mouldering red robes. A black hood trimmed with skeletal insignia identify him to have once been an acolyte of Vashna. He and his brothers were attacked, robbed, and murdered by the brigands when they passed this way some weeks earlier. This clearing is where they disposed of the bodies.

If you wish to search the robes of this corpse, turn to **199**.

If you wish to leave this crude graveyard and return to the trail, turn to **156**.

### 343

As the acolyte immediately before you in the line steps into the arch, your sixth sense screams a warning of imminent danger.

If you wish to ignore your Kai senses and step through the arch, turn to **130**.

If you decide to follow your senses and refuse to step through the arch, turn to **28**.

## 344

You are awoken in the middle of the night by the she-cat's nervous growl. At first you think that a new day must already have dawned for the cave is awash with bright light, but when you look out at the surrounding landscape you see that the light has a far more sinister origin.

The sky is alive with hordes of glowing, wraith-like phantoms. They swoop down from the roiling storm clouds and skim the tree-tops, howling and screeching like angry banshees. A trio of these ghastly apparitions passes within a few yards of the cave mouth and startle the wild cat and her mewing cub. Terrified, they flee the cave and disappear into the pines.

If you possess Kai-screen, and have attained the rank of Kai Grand Guardian or higher, turn to **283**.

If you do not possess Kai-screen, or have yet to attain this Kai rank, turn to **19**.

## 345

Time passes and you sense flashing motes of light streaking past your closed eyes, and faint far away sounds come dimly to your ears through the howling wind. Then, as suddenly as it began, the sensation of falling ceases and you feel yourself lurching forwards on to wet, rocky soil. Rain spatters your face and, when you open your eyes, you see that you have returned to Magnamund . . . and to terrible danger.

'Kill him!' It is the voice of Arch Druid Cadak. You have emerged from the shadow gate and now you

XX. A growling horde of vengeful acolytes close in upon
you.

lie on the ground between the great shimmering arch and Cadak's crystal dais. You have only just found your feet when a growling horde of vengeful acolytes close in upon you, eager to fulfil their leader's wish.

Acolytes of Vashna:
COMBAT SKILL 40   ENDURANCE 45

If you choose to use the Deathstaff as your weapon during this fight, you may add 10 to your COMBAT SKILL.

If you win the combat (using the Deathstaff), turn to **26**.

If you win the combat (without using the Death-staff), turn to **324**.

### 346

Using your formidable mind skill, you create a protective wall around your will which deflects the woman's psychic power-charm. Her spell rebounds and the suddenness of this reversal completely overwhelms her senses. In an instant the light vanishes from her eyes and her face becomes blank and expressionless, like that of a mask of a mindless automaton.

Turn to **115**.

### 347

You slay all but one jackal. This bruised and blood-spattered cur flees from the shore, defeated but determined not to suffer the fate of the others. You pause to wipe the sticky gore from your weapon, then you mount your horse and set off along the rugged shoreline, foregoing the shelter of the horseshoe boulders in case the jackal should return in the night with more of its ferocious brothers.

Fortunately, you soon reach firmer ground and, by nightfall, you come to a sheltered cove where you find a warm hollow in which to set up camp for the night. Unless you possess Grand Huntmastery, you must now eat a Meal or lose 3 ENDURANCE points.

To continue, turn to **296**.

### 348

As the last of the Vakovarians falls dead at your feet, you step away from their heaped bodies and wipe the sweat of battle from your bloodied brow. You have slain the enemy but you can hear more of their kind stumbling across the boulders, eager to reach you and avenge the deaths of their brothers-in-arms.

You retreat into the copse, using your Magnakai skills of invisibility to keep you hidden from the advancing brigands. In their clumsy eagerness to enter the trees, they fail to notice you slip through their lines and circle around behind them. You have outwitted them but you are still anxious that they may find your horse. You move to higher ground in order to get a better view of the copse and, from a vantage point among the boulders, you observe their leader and three of his henchmen hiding nearby, crouched behind the bough of a fallen tree.

If you possess a Bow and wish to fire an arrow at the Brigand leader, turn to **304**.

If you possess Kai-alchemy and wish to use the spell 'Mind Charm', turn to **212**.

If you decide to wait and observe these brigands a little longer, turn to **98**.

### 349

As you approach the trough, you feel the token getting hotter in your pocket. Your Magnakai skill of Nexus protects you from the heat, yet it does not prevent the glowing token from setting your tunic alight. Immediately you smother the flames but the resulting smoke causes a commotion among the acolytes following behind.

If you possess Kai-alchemy, and wish to use it, turn to **86**.

If you possess Grand Huntmastery and have attained the rank of Sun Lord, and wish to use your Discipline, turn to **237**.

If you have neither of the above, or choose not to use them, turn to **186**.

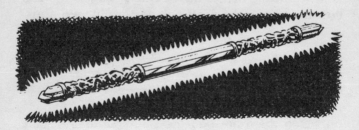

### 350

Suddenly, the raging winds cease and you fall unconscious to the floor of the dais. When you awaken you discover that you are entirely alone. The collapse of the shadow gate and the whirlwind which followed have consumed everything, save yourself and the crystal dais: no acolytes, no trace of the grand archway, no Deathstaff, not even the storms remain. Virtually all trace of Cadak's evil plan has been wiped from the surface of your world.

Congratulations, Grand Master Lone Wolf. You have triumphed. You have defeated the plan to resurrect Vashna and saved Magnamund from his rule of terror. But the fight against Evil is not yet over. The collapsing shadow gate destroyed everything it consumed . . . everything, that is, with one exception. That exception returns to haunt you in the next Grand Master adventure, entitled:

THE DEATHLORD OF IXIA

# RANDOM NUMBER TABLE

| 8 | 4 | 6 | 1 | 0 | 5 | 6 | 8 | 3 | 2 |
|---|---|---|---|---|---|---|---|---|---|
| 0 | 6 | 3 | 6 | 0 | 5 | 8 | 7 | 4 | 9 |
| 7 | 5 | 6 | 2 | 5 | 8 | 4 | 8 | 1 | 6 |
| 5 | 3 | 4 | 7 | 6 | 5 | 8 | 5 | 0 | 9 |
| 0 | 1 | 9 | 6 | 2 | 9 | 8 | 3 | 1 | 8 |
| 2 | 7 | 1 | 4 | 1 | 2 | 7 | 4 | 8 | 5 |
| 1 | 0 | 6 | 7 | 8 | 0 | 2 | 3 | 1 | 0 |
| 6 | 8 | 0 | 2 | 4 | 9 | 5 | 6 | 2 | 9 |
| 5 | 4 | 8 | 7 | 8 | 5 | 2 | 7 | 0 | 8 |
| 1 | 6 | 3 | 2 | 9 | 4 | 1 | 4 | 5 | 7 |